D1308113

TEKNON
AND THE
CHAMPION
WARRIORS

Mission Guide

AN INTERACTIVE ADVENTURE TO EXPLORE COURAGEOUS MANHOOD

A companion study guide for
Teknon and the Champion Warriors

A *Mentor Guide* for dads and
leaders is also available

Teknon and the CHAMPION Warriors Mission Guide–Son

© 2000, 2006 Brent Sapp. All rights reserved.

No part of this book may be reproduced, stored in a retrieval system, or transmitted in any form or by any means electronic, mechanical, photocopying, recording, or otherwise, without prior permission from the publisher.

Published by Generations of Virtue

Author: Brent Sapp
Senior Editor: Ben Colter and Julie Hiramine
Editorial Team: Stephen W. Sorenson, Anne Wooten, Fran Taylor, David Sims,
            Bob Anderson, Megan Briggs, Katherine Lockhart, and Sara Raley
Illustrator: Sergio Cariello
Designer: Jerry McCall and David Rhody

ISBN 0-9766143-8-3
Printed in the United States of America.

Most of the content of the Just Do It! appendix is taken from *Would You Like to Know God Personally?* a version of the *Four Spiritual Laws*, written by Bill Bright. Copyright © 1965, 1968, Campus Crusade for Christ, Inc. All rights reserved.

Most Scripture quotations are taken from the New American Standard Bible.
© 1960, 1962, 1963, 1968, 1971, 1972, 1973, 1975, 1977, 1994 by The Lockman Foundation.   All rights reserved. Used by permission.

The following Bible versions are also used:

NIV—Scripture quotations marked (NIV) are taken from The Holy Bible, New International Version®. NIV®. Copyright © 1973, 1978, 1984 by International Bible Society. Used by permission of Zondervan Publishing House. All rights reserved.

TLB—Verses marked (TLB) are taken from The Living Bible © 1971. Used by permission of Tyndale House Publishers, Inc., Wheaton, IL 60189. All rights reserved.

NOTE: This book is intended for boys ages 11 to 16. However, it contains some mature
        subject matter addressing dating, sexual temptation, and pornography.

P.O. Box 62253
Colorado Springs, CO 80962
www.generationsofvirtue.org

*The CHAMPION Training
adventure program
is dedicated to a pair of champions—
my mom and dad*

TEKNON AND THE CHAMPION WARRIORS

Mission Guide

An Interactive Adventure to Explore Courageous Manhood

TABLE OF CONTENTS

Vital Documents

What Is a CHAMPION Warrior? 3

CHAMPION Warrior Creed 5

CHAMPION Code 6

The Map of the Mission 8

CHAMPION Sheet of Deeds 9

CHAMPION Sessions

Session 1   Destination: Kairos 11

Session 2A   My Enemy, Your Enemy Part 1 21

Session 2B   My Enemy, Your Enemy Part 2 31

Session 3   The Second Look 41

Session 4   The Company I Keep 53

Session 5   Ergonian Pride 63

Session 6   A Storm of Dishonor 73

Session 7   An Excellent Choice 83

Session 8   Faced With Fear 99

Session 9   Recover, Recover, Recover 111

Session 10   Good Enough 123

Session 11   The Element of Doubt 137

Session 12   Nothing More, Nothing Less, Nothing Else 149

Session 13   A Job to Finish 161

Session 14   Back to Back 173

Session 15   Celebration 187

Appendix A: Just Do It! 198

Appendix B: The CHAMPION Training Program 202

Appendix C: Media Evaluation Report 203

Acknowledgements and Notes 204

About the Author and Illustrator 205

What is a
Champion Warrior?

What comes to mind when you hear the word *warrior*? Today, that word refers to many things, like the road warrior who just invested his entire savings into an overpriced motorcycle and dominates the road. Or the weekend warrior, an overstuffed couch potato who sits in an overstuffed chair, watching whatever stuff ESPN is showing all weekend long. And what comes to mind when you hear the word *champion*? Do you think of the guy who won several gold medals in the Olympics? Or the winner of the Indy 500? Those definitions may be true, but they bear little resemblance to the real warriors and champions of years past.

Many years ago, Native Americans living on the Western plains rode on horseback into battle when they reached their 14th birthday. A boy trained with his father early in life so that he could assume responsibility, take care of others, and, if necessary, fight to protect the safety of the tribe. These sons were more than teenagers; they were young men, each with the *soul of a warrior*.

In July 1776, General George Washington led his 5,000 troops, many under the age of 15, into battle against 25,000 of the finest soldiers Great Britain had to offer. Washington's outnumbered armed forces courageously held their position and played a vital role in gaining the freedom Americans enjoy today. These brave soldiers were more than teenagers; they were young men, each with the *heart of a champion*.

Since those days, many in our society have lost the vision for developing courageous young men. As a result, young men have not been given the responsibility they are capable of taking on. Many have not been challenged to think big thoughts and dream big dreams. How about you? Are you infected with the venom of low expectations or are you setting high standards for yourself? What are your values? What are your goals? Are you living a life full of challenge, adventure, and fulfillment?

How would you like to become a young man with the soul of a warrior and the heart of a champion? You can! Are you ready to begin the quest toward courageous manhood? Are you willing to invest the time and energy? If so, the CHAMPION Training adventure is for you!

Your *Mission Guide* includes 16 CHAMPION Sessions that you will complete and then discuss with your dad or leader over the course of several months. You will probably meet together every other week.

Elements of a CHAMPION Session

▲ **CHAMPION Characteristics**—One or two key character traits are highlighted for each session.

▲ **Discussion Topics**—Key subjects you will address in the session are summarized.

▲ **Mission Debrief**—Debriefing is a military practice where a soldier recaps his previous mission activities. This section provides you an opportunity to review with your dad the mission that was assigned at your previous session. You will debrief on your critical maneuver, your action point from the Sheet of Deeds, and the new power verse you memorized.

▲ **Reconnaissance**—Reconnaissance (or "recon") is also a military activity in which a soldier explores an area to gather important information for the mission ahead. In this section you and your dad will discuss an episode from *Teknon and the CHAMPION Warriors*.

▲ **Strategy and Tactics**—Strategy refers to the overall planning of a mission. Tactics refers to the methods used to secure the objectives planned out in the strategy. In this section you and your dad will discuss specific CHAMPION characteristics, investigate strategies and tactics from the Bible, and discover how to apply them in your life.

▲ **Your Mission**—At the end of each CHAMPION Session, your dad will assign a mission to you to be completed before the next session. Each mission includes:

   ■ **Power Verse:** A new Bible verse related to the session for you to memorize.

   ■ **Critical Maneuver:** A fun, hands-on project or activity for you and your dad to do together to reinforce what you discussed during your session (movies, interviews, tally surveys, Bible discovery, books, and more movies!).

   ■ **CHAMPION Sheet of Deeds:** You and your dad will agree on an action point that you will begin to apply before the next session and that you will carry on as you develop these deeds for a lifetime as a CHAMPION.

Get ready for a challenging experience that will change your life!

COURAGE · HONOR · ATTITUDE · MENTAL TOUGHNESS · PURITY · INTEGRITY · OWNERSHIP · NAVIGATION

THE CHAMPION
WARRIOR CREED

"IF I HAVE THE COURAGE TO FACE MY FEARS; HONOR, WHICH I SHOW TO GOD* AND MY FELLOW MAN; THE PROPER ATTITUDE CONCERNING MYSELF AND MY CIRCUMSTANCES; THE MENTAL TOUGHNESS REQUIRED TO MAKE HARD DECISIONS; PURITY OF HEART, MIND, AND BODY; THE INTEGRITY TO STAND FOR WHAT I BELIEVE, EVEN IN THE MOST DIFFICULT SITUATIONS; EFFECTIVE OWNERSHIP OF ALL THAT IS ENTRUSTED TO ME; AND FOCUSED NAVIGATION IN ORDER TO SUCCESSFULLY CHART MY COURSE IN LIFE; I WILL LIVE AS A TRUE CHAMPION WARRIOR, COMMITTED TO BATTLING EVIL, AND CHANGING MY WORLD FOR GOD'S GLORY."

* Note: In the fiction book, *Teknon and the CHAMPION Warriors*, the Warrior King called Pneuma is a fictional character intended to represent God (Father, Son, and Holy Spirit). For this study, the name Pneuma is only used when referring to the fictional story character.

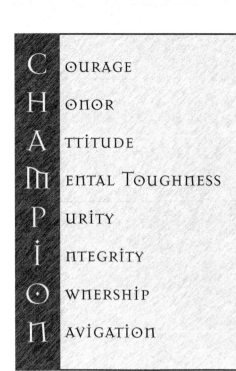

C OURAGE

H ONOR

A TTITUDE

M ENTAL TOUGHNESS

P URITY

I NTEGRITY

O WNERSHIP

N AVIGATION

THE CHAMPION CODE

Character is the moral strength that grows out of our relationship with God.* Personal growth is expressed through the physical, emotional, social, mental, and especially spiritual areas of our lives.

Characteristics of a CHAMPION Warrior

COURAGE

I will cultivate bravery and trust in God. I will break out of my comfort zone by seeking to conquer my fears. I will learn to recover, recover, and recover again.

HONOR

I will honor God by obeying Him and acknowledging Him as the complete source of my life, both now and through eternity. I will treat my parents, siblings, friends, and acquaintances with respect. I will appreciate the strengths and accept the weaknesses of all my "team members."

ATTITUDE

I will cultivate a disposition of humility. I will assume a correct and hopeful view of myself as a member of God's family. I will improve my ability to manage anger and discouragement. I will develop and enjoy an appropriate sense of humor.

Mental Toughness

I will allow God to direct my thinking toward gaining common sense and wisdom. I will use discernment when making hard decisions. I will desire respect from others rather than compromise my convictions for acceptance or approval.

Purity

I will train myself to keep the temple of my body and mind uncorrupted mentally, emotionally, and physically. I commit to avoid and flee sexual temptation.

Integrity

I will seek to acquire a clear understanding of who I am in Christ so that I may have a deeper comprehension of what I believe, what I stand for, and how I can live out those convictions in the most difficult circumstances, whether I am alone or with others. I will allow other people to hold me accountable to standards of excellence.

Ownership

I will apply effective stewardship by using my life and the resources God entrusts to me—including my possessions, time, and talents—for His glory. I will seek contentment in God's provision for my needs. I will learn to practice delayed gratification.

Navigation

I will allow God to chart my course by accepting my mission from Him, and I will complete that mission by trusting in Him. I will study the Bible, God's Word, so I can know Him better and gain His strength and direction for my life. I will become goal-oriented by learning to focus my attention on completing worthwhile short-term and long-term objectives.

*Note: In the fiction book, *Teknon and the CHAMPION Warriors*, the Warrior King called Pneuma is a fictional character intended to represent God (Father, Son, and Holy Spirit). For this study, the name Pneuma is only used when referring to the fictional story character.

The Map of the Mission

TEKNON AND THE CHAMPION WARRIORS

The CHAMPION Sheet of Deeds

Following are my personal action points for each session of my CHAMPION Training. I will strive to apply these action points during my training adventure and also will make an effort to continue applying them as I seek to grow in godly character for a lifetime of living as a CHAMPION.

Session 1: _____

Session 2A: _____

Session 2B: _____

Session 3: _____

Session 4: _____

Session 5: _____

Session 6: _____

Session 7: _____

Session 8: _____

Session 9: _____

Session 10: _____

Session 11: _____

Session 12: _____

Session 13: _____

Session 14: _____

Session 15: _____

TEKNON AND THE CHAMPION WARRIORS

COURAGE • HONOR • ATTITUDE • MENTAL TOUGHNESS • PURITY • INTEGRITY • OWNERSHIP • NAVIGATION

SESSION 1:
DESTINATION: KAIROS

CHAMPION Characteristics

Courage and Navigation

POWER VERSE: PHILIPPIANS 4:6-7

Be anxious for nothing, but in everything by prayer and supplication with thanksgiving let your requests be made known to God. And the peace of God, which surpasses all comprehension, will guard your hearts and your minds in Christ Jesus.

Preparing for a challenging task
Overcoming fear of the unknown
Accepting my responsibility and trusting God with the rest

Mission Debrief

1. Normally, this section will be used to debrief together about how your mission assignment from the previous session went.

2. Read the CHAMPION Warrior Creed out loud together (see page 5).

Reconnaissance

1. Carefully review the Map of the Mission on page 8 before beginning this section. Identify where the team is located in episode 1.

2a. What is the CHAMPION definition of **Courage**? Of **Navigation**? (Refer to the CHAMPION Code on page 6.)

_____

_____

_____

_____

_____

Do the thing you fear, and fear will die.

Anonymous

3. What opportunity do you think the team has before them on the planet Kairos?

_____

_____

4. Why do you think Teknon was nervous about this mission?

_____

_____

Optional Questions

5. What kind of training do you think Teknon undertook to prepare for this journey?

_____

_____

6. What do you think Teknon's responsibilities were as he prepared physically, mentally, and spiritually for this mission?

_____

_____

7. As the team members stood on the assimilator platform, Kratos said, "... no man is worthy who is not ready at all times to risk body, status, and life itself for a great cause." What do you think Kratos meant? What kind of cause do you think he was talking about?

_____

_____

There lives in each of us a hero, awaiting a call to action.

H. Jackson Brown, Jr.

8. How would you apply Kratos' advice to Teknon: "It's all right to be nervous. The trick is learning to channel that nervous energy into something productive"?

_____

_____

Strategy and Tactics

1. Review Philippians 4:6-7. What do these verses say about fear or anxiety? How can we face our fears and be at peace?

_____

_____

_____

Accept the challenges so that you may feel the exhilaration of victory.

General George S. Patton

Taking Responsibility

In 1917, Will Stoneman gathered all of his courage as he stepped out of the train and into the frigid Canadian air of Winnipeg, Manitoba. He gazed for a moment at the bright lights and endless activity. At age 17, this rugged farm boy from the hills of South Dakota was about to undertake the greatest challenge of his life. In a few short hours, he would begin a 500-mile dog sled race in hopes of winning the $10,000 first prize.

Will needed the money to save his family's farm and pay for his college education. His father had died in a sledding accident only a few weeks earlier, leaving the family without the income from their cabinet-making trade. Now Will was alone in a big city, about to race against the finest sled teams in the world over some of the roughest territory in North America.

What would most teenagers have said if they were faced with Will's challenge?

What can I do? I'm just a teenager.

It's too late for me to make a difference now.

Even if I tried, I'd probably drop out the first day, so I won't bother.

I don't have the experience. Why can't somebody else race for our family?

Will Stoneman didn't choose to make excuses. He saw an opportunity to help his family, and he jumped at it. He courageously took responsibility to compete in a difficult race, even though he had only a month to prepare for it. During that month, he worked as hard as he could, training himself to race on little food and even less sleep than any of his competitors. He did everything within his ability to contribute to his family's success.

His determination shocked the entire country when, against incredible odds, he won the race! His unwillingness to give up, regardless of the circumstances, earned him the nickname "Iron Will."

2. Read James 1:22-26. What happens if we only listen to the Word and do nothing? (See verse 22.)

_____

_____

3. What will happen to the person who takes responsibility to do what the Word says? (See verse 25.)

_____

_____

_____

_____

GOD'S RING

CHAMPION's RING

THE CHAMPION's RING

Notice that the Hoplon shield has two rings on it. These circles represent the CHAMPION Warrior's Rings of Responsibility in life. The inner ring is the CHAMPION's Ring, which symbolizes the behaviors and activities in which the CHAMPION can make a difference by obeying God. Inside this ring, a CHAMPION completes his responsibilities without grumbling and without blaming other people for the choices he makes.

A CHAMPION regularly reads the Bible and prays for direction so that he can know how God wants him to think and act. He trusts God to give him the power to make the best choices, while at the same time taking responsibility to do everything he can to live like a CHAMPION.

When we obey God and courageously take responsibility for our choices and actions, we move a step closer toward becoming CHAMPIONs.

4. What are some behaviors and activities that should go into the CHAMPION's Ring?

_____

_____

_____

5. In what areas do you need to assume more responsibility in your life? Be specific!

_____

_____

God's Ring

There are also times when a CHAMPION should not attempt to assume responsibility. Look at the outer ring of the Hoplon. This section of the shield represents God's Ring.

6. Read Psalm 28:7-8. Where does the strength of a CHAMPION come from?

_____

_____

7. Read John 15:4-5. What do you think it means to abide (some Bible translations say "remain") in Christ?

_____

_____

_____

8. What can we accomplish if we don't abide in Christ?

_____

_____

_____

_____

Let me assert my firm belief, that the only thing to fear is fear itself.

Franklin D. Roosevelt

"Have I not commanded you? Be strong and courageous. Do not tremble or be dismayed, for the Lord your God is with you wherever you go."

Joshua 1:9

A CHAMPION takes responsibility for his actions, but everything else in life is God's responsibility and remains in God's Ring. If we obey God and seek Him daily, He will take care of us in every way.

9. Read Joshua 1:9. Why should we be strong and courageous?

_____

_____

_____

10. Name one thing that you worry about, something you currently keep in the CHAMPION's Ring that really should be placed into God's Ring.

_____

_____

_____

_____

_____

God's Ring encircles the CHAMPION's Ring because God is constantly with us, and His love surrounds us wherever we are. It is God's responsibility to watch over us and protect us. In fact, the Bible tells us that God is our shield (Psalm 28:7).

God is even responsible for paying for our failures and sins. Only He can give us eternal life through His Son, Jesus Christ. When we receive Jesus into our lives, we are given a special relationship as a son in God's family and covered by the protection of His all-powerful love.

If you don't yet have this kind of personal relationship with God, but would like to be under His love and protection, turn to the section entitled Just Do It! in the Appendix.

THE Main Things I learned in this Champion Session are:

_____

_____

_____

_____

_____

There are times when obedient acts of self-sacrifice and courage merit both admiration and profound gratitude.

William Bennett

CHAMPION
Sheet of Deeds

Go to the CHAMPION Sheet of Deeds on page 9 and write down **one thing you will do** in the upcoming days (and beyond) to apply the main things you learned in session 1.

◆ Session 1 ◆

19

Your Mission

Complete your mission and CHAMPION Session prep before you meet for session 2A.

Power Verse: Philippians 4:6-7

Date memorized: _____

Critical Maneuver

This will reinforce what you learned today. Obtain your manuever instructions from your father.

CHAMPION Sheet of Deeds

Begin to apply your action point from your Sheet of Deeds.

CHAMPION Session Prep

Reread episode 2 of *Teknon and the CHAMPION Warriors*, and then complete the questions in session 2A of your *Mission Guide* on your own. **Our next CHAMPION Session will be:**

DATE:

_____

TIME:

_____

PLACE:

_____

COURAGE • HONOR • ATTITUDE • MENTAL TOUGHNESS • PURITY • INTEGRITY • OWNERSHIP • NAVIGATION

SESSION 2A:
MY ENEMY, YOUR ENEMY

CHAMPION Characteristics
Mental Toughness and Navigation

POWER VERSE: JAMES 4:7-8A

Submit therefore to God. Resist the devil and he will flee from you.
Draw near to God and He will draw near to you.

Discussion Topics

Assessing the enemy
Embracing the mission you have been given
Learning to defeat the enemy

Mission Debrief

1. Discuss your mission from session 1. Did you complete your maneuver? If so, what did you learn? If not, why not?

2. Did you start applying your first action point from your Sheet of Deeds? If so, what did you learn? Have you had any struggles in trying to apply it?

3. Recite your memory verse (Philippians 4:6-7) from session 1.

4. Read the CHAMPION Warrior Creed out loud together again (see page 5).

Reconnaissance

1. Carefully review the Map of the Mission on page 8 before beginning this section. Identify where the team is located in episode 2.

2. What is the CHAMPION definition of **Mental Toughness**? Of **Navigation**? (Refer to the CHAMPION Code on page 6.)

_____

_____

_____

_____

Nearly all men can stand adversity, but if you want to test a man's character, give him power.

Abraham Lincoln

3. In this episode, Kratos describes the team's primary enemy. Who is he and why is he so dangerous? What is he trying to do?

_____

_____

_____

_____

_____

4. Who is the team's secondary enemy created by Magos? What is his function?

_____

_____

_____

_____

5. Why does Magos want to defeat Kratos?

_____

_____

6. What did Magos steal? Why did he steal it? Why did Kratos want to get it back?

_____

_____

7. Why did Kratos refuse to be recreated and join Magos?

_____

_____

8. What did Kratos mean when he said, "Where there is no character, there is no threat to Magos."

_____

_____

9. The Greek word *artios*, refers to something that is complete and fitted perfectly. What does Artios (Arti) do to live up to his name?

_____

_____

_____

_____

Strategy and Tactics

Enemy Assessment

A hunter in the wilderness aimed at a bear with his gun. Suddenly the bear shouted, "Why do you want to shoot me?"

The hunter replied, "I need a fur coat for the winter."

The bear responded, "Well, all I want is a good breakfast. Why don't we sit down and discuss our needs?"

The hunter thought for a minute, then sat down and discussed the issue with the bear. After a short time, the only one left was the bear, who did indeed enjoy a good breakfast. The hunter ended up with a fur coat, but not at all in the way he had planned. In other words, the hunter let his guard down at the wrong time.

In the same way, Kratos knew he could not join Magos, or even discuss joining him. Kratos hated everything that his former partner wanted to accomplish. To join Magos, Kratos would have had to become like the cyborg, almost a part of the enemy he sought to defeat. Kratos realized he could not let his guard down for a minute with his enemy.

Who Is Your Enemy?

Did you know that the Bible says you have an enemy? And did you realize that you should hate this enemy and everything that he stands for? Your enemy is Satan, also known as the devil. At one time, Satan was an angel, part of God's heavenly host (Isaiah 14:12-15, Luke 11:14-23).

But Satan became prideful and actually challenged God's authority. Like Magos, who chose to transform himself, Satan took matters into his own hands and allowed his pride to direct his actions. He wanted to become something he was not. He wanted to become God. As a result, God kicked him out of heaven forever.

When Satan was cast out, many of the other angels joined him in his rebellion. These angels now serve him around the world, which is currently in his control (1 John 5:19), by tempting, seducing, and enticing us to disobey God. Just like Scandalon is serving Magos, these angels serve Satan in his evil schemes.

Satan hates you and everything about you because he hates God. If you have invited Christ into your life, you are going to spend eternity with Christ in heaven. That is something Satan will never be able to do. Satan's mission is to ruin as many people as he can. He wants to accomplish his mission before Christ comes back again to rule forever.

1. Read 1 Peter 5:8. What does the Bible say that Satan wants to do to us?

_____

_____

_____

2. How should we respond to Satan's plan for us?

_____

_____

_____

_____

_____

_____

_____

◆ Teknon and the CHAMPION Warriors ◆

Satan wants to infect our thoughts, our desires, and our actions so that we will be ineffective for God. If you are a Christian, Satan can't prevent you from going to heaven, but he can make your life ineffective and miserable if you allow him to do so. What's worse, he will use your poor choices, ineffectiveness, and disobedience to display you as a poor example of God's sons to the world.

3. What do you think Satan would like for us to think about?

_____

_____

Remember, Satan is a brilliant enemy (see Ephesians 6:10-18). Never underestimate him. He knows what tempts you and then plots to bring those temptations into your path. Every time you make a decision in obedience to God, Satan loses. Every time you make a wrong decision, like telling a lie or cheating on a test, he leaves you to deal with the consequences and brings a more serious temptation into your path, hoping you will make the wrong decision again.

But there's good news! God knows that Satan is your enemy. Your Heavenly Father wants to provide all of the strength you need to defeat Satan every day. Through Jesus' death, burial, and resurrection, He has defeated the devil (Genesis 3:15) and has overcome the world (John 16:33). All you have to do is put your trust in Christ and obey His instructions to be victorious.

DEFEATING THE ENEMY

4. Read James 4:7-8. What does the Bible say to do to the devil to make him flee from you?

_____

_____

_____

My message to you is: Be courageous! ... Be as brave as your fathers before you. Have faith! Go forward.

Thomas A. Edison

5. Why is it important for us to admit that Satan has influence in this world?

_____

_____

6. Should we fear Satan? Why or why not?

_____

_____

_____

The Bible also says, "Greater is He [Christ] who is in you than he who is in the world [Satan]." You must realize that Satan is a formidable enemy, but you do not need to fear him. If you are a Christian, you belong to Almighty God, so He will give you guidance and protection. God also assigns His angels to us; they are charged with guarding those who fear and follow Him (Psalm 34:7, 91:11).

7. What can you do to protect yourself according to God's instructions in Psalm 119:9-11?

_____

_____

_____

_____

_____

_____

_____

"Have I not commanded you? Be strong and courageous! Do not tremble or be dismayed, for the Lord your God is with you wherever you go."

Joshua 1:9

The Main Things I learned
in this Champion Session are:

_____

_____

_____

_____

_____

Champion
Sheet of Deeds

Go to the CHAMPION Sheet of Deeds on page 9 and write down **one thing you will begin to do** before the next session (and beyond) to apply the main things you learned in session 2A.

Your Mission

Complete your mission and CHAMPION Session Prep before you meet for session 2B.

POWER VERSE: JAMES 4:7-8A

Date memorized: _____

CRITICAL MANEUVER

This will reinforce what you learned today. Obtain your maneuver instructions from your father.

CHAMPION SHEET OF DEEDS

Begin to apply your action point from your Sheet of Deeds.

CHAMPION SESSION PREP

Reread episode 2 of *Teknon and the CHAMPION Warriors*, and then complete the questions in session 2B in your *Mission Guide* on your own. **Our next CHAMPION Session will be:**

DATE:

_____

TIME:

_____

PLACE:

_____

COURAGE · HONOR · ATTITUDE · MENTAL TOUGHNESS · PURITY · INTEGRITY · OWNERSHIP · NAVIGATION

SESSION · 2B:
MY ENEMY, YOUR ENEMY

CHAMPION Characteristic

Ownership

POWER VERSE: LUKE 16:10 (NIV)

Whoever can be trusted with very little can also be trusted with much, and whoever is dishonest with very little will also be dishonest with much.

Discussion Topics

Learning that God owns all things
Becoming an effective steward of our resources

Mission Debrief

1. Discuss your mission from session 2A. Did you complete your maneuver? If so, what did you learn? If not, why not?

2. Did you start applying your new action point from your Sheet of Deeds? How are these action points affecting your mindset?

3. Recite your power verse (James 4:7-8a) from session 2B.

4. Read the CHAMPION Warrior Creed out loud together again (see page 5).

Reconnaissance

1. Carefully review the Map of the Mission on page 8 before beginning this section. Identify where the team is located in episode 2.

◆ Teknon and the CHAMPION Warriors ◆

2. What is the CHAMPION definition of **Ownership**? (Refer to the CHAMPION Code on page 6.)

_____

_____

_____

_____

3. Why did Teknon buy the Shocktech?

_____

_____

_____

4. Did Teknon need the Shocktech? Why or why not?

_____

_____

_____

5a. Was Teknon free to spend his money the way he chose to spend it?

_____

_____

_____

_____

5b. Was Teknon wise in the spending choice he made? Why?

_____

_____

6. What did Kratos recommend to Teknon about spending money?

_____

_____

_____

_____

7. What do you think is the difference between a need and a want?

_____

_____

_____

8. Kratos said, "You can splurge once in a while, but give yourself enough time to think about it before you make the purchase." What items are you tempted to buy impulsively?

_____

_____

_____

_____

Strategy and Tactics

Effective Stewardship

1. Is it wrong to spend money? Absolutely not, but God wants us to spend it wisely. Did you know there are more verses in the Bible concerning money than on almost any other subject? Why do you think there are so many verses about money?

    _____

    _____

    Money is a tool God has given each of us to use and to manage. The way you manage money often reflects what you think about Who provided it to you. Managing money is a visible expression of your relationship with God—your values and your trust in Him.

2. What can happen when a family gets into the habit of spending money on the spur of the moment like Teknon did?

    _____

    _____

3. Ecclesiastes was written by King Solomon, one of the richest people who ever lived. Solomon had more money than he could spend, although the Bible says he spent quite a bit. What does Ecclesiastes 2:10-11 say about spending money?

    _____

    _____

    _____

    _____

Solomon realized that he shouldn't have been so frivolous and irresponsible in his spending. Likewise, whether you have a lot of money or a little money, God expects you to use it wisely. When you do that, you are considered a good steward or manager.

4. According to Matthew 25:14-30, how much money did the owner give each servant? How did he decide what to give each one?

_____

_____

_____

5. What did the owner want the servants to do with the money?

_____

_____

_____

6. Which servants were good stewards?

_____

_____

_____

7. What do you think is the difference between an owner and a steward?

_____

_____

_____

When prosperity comes, do not use all of it.

Benjamin Franklin

God is the owner of all good and perfect things on this earth. We are His stewards. What a privilege we have to be entrusted by God with His resources! God doesn't mind if you spend money. He may not even mind if you occasionally spend money on something you really want that you really don't need. But that should be the exception, not the rule.

Remember, God owns it all—our time, our talent, our possessions, and our money. He entrusts them to us. Think about what you buy before you buy it. Don't buy on the spur of the moment. Think and pray for wisdom before you make a big purchase. Seek wise counsel from others who are good stewards.

8. How can you become a good steward of your money and possessions?

_____

_____

_____

_____

_____

Be a good steward of everything that God entrusts to you. And remember, never spend more than 100 specas for a Shocktech!

Beware of little expenses. A small leak will sink a great ship.

Benjamin Franklin

The Main Things I learned in this Champion Session are:

_____

_____

_____

_____

_____

_____

> *So often we spend money we don't have, on things we don't need, to impress other people we don't even like.*
>
> Sam Bartlett

CHAMPION
Sheet of Deeds

Go to the CHAMPION Sheet of Deeds on page 9 and write down **one thing you will begin to do** before the next session (and beyond) to apply the main things you learned in session 2B.

◆ Teknon and the CHAMPION Warriors ◆

Your Mission

Complete your mission and CHAMPION Session Prep before you meet for session 3.

Power Verse: Luke 16:10

Date memorized: _____

Critical Maneuver

This will reinforce what you learned today. Obtain your maneuver instructions from your father.

CHAMPION Sheet of Deeds

Begin to apply your action point from your Sheet of Deeds.

CHAMPION Session Prep

Reread episode 3 of *Teknon and the CHAMPION Warriors*, and then complete the questions in session 3 in your *Mission Guide* on your own. **Our next CHAMPION Session will be:**

DATE:

_____

TIME:

_____

PLACE:

_____

Courage • Honor • Attitude • Mental toughness • Purity • Integrity • Ownership • Navigation

Session 3:
The Second Look

CHAMPION Characteristic

Purity

POWER VERSE: 1 Corinthians 6:18

Flee immorality. Every other sin that a man commits is outside the body, but the immoral man sins against his own body.

Discussion Topics

Understanding the right context for sex
Establishing boundaries in physical intimacy
Setting high standards to guard your purity

Mission Debrief

1. Discuss your mission from session 2B. What did you learn from your maneuver? How is what you've learned affecting your thinking or behavior?

    _____

    _____

2. Did you start applying your new action point from your Sheet of Deeds? Any progress to report? Any struggles?

    _____

    _____

3. Recite your power verse (Luke 16:10) from session 2B.

4. What are a few things that God has entrusted to you (for example: money, talents, time) that require good stewardship? How will you be a faithful steward?

    _____

    _____

5. Recite as much as you can of the CHAMPION Warrior Creed from memory (see page 5).

RECONNAISSANCE

1. Review the Map of the Mission on page 8 and determine the team's location in episode 3.

2. What is the CHAMPION definition of **Purity**? (Refer to the CHAMPION Code on page 6.)

   _____

   _____

   _____

3. Why do you think Scandalon tempted Teknon?

   _____

   _____

   _____

   _____

4. When should Teknon have returned to camp? Why?

   _____

   _____

   _____

   _____

   _____

5. What did Teknon mean when he said, "I guess I shouldn't have taken the second look"?

_____

_____

_____

6a. What did Kratos mean when he said, "Error increases with distance"?

_____

_____

_____

6b. How does that insight relate to physical and sexual intimacy?

_____

_____

7. What point did Kratos want to make by mentioning the story of the transtron racer and the cliff?

_____

_____

_____

_____

8. Why do you think Kratos suggested that Teknon wait until marriage to kiss a woman?

_____

_____

_____

9. How did Teknon react to the idea of the Wedding Kiss?

_____

_____

Let us not lose heart in doing good, for in due time we will reap if we do not grow weary. So then, while we have opportunity, let us do good to all people, and especially to those who are of the household of the faith.

Galatians 6:9-10

Optional Questions

10. Kratos said, "If a couple will wait to experience sex in the correct setting of marriage, they will receive incredible benefits of trust, bonding, and sheer enjoyment. However, if sex is misused, many long-term problems can occur." What kind of problems is he talking about?

_____

_____

11. What do you think Kratos meant when he said, "Once you take a step closer to the edge [physical intimacy], it's very difficult to take a step back"?

_____

_____

_____

Strategy and Tactics

Right Time, Right Place, Right Person

I have been crucified with Christ; and it is no longer I who live, but Christ lives in me; and the life which I now live in the flesh I live by faith in the Son of God, who loved me and gave Himself up for me.

Galatians 2:20

   While leading a discussion on the topic of sexual purity with a class of engaged couples, the teacher explored the importance of waiting until marriage to have sexual intimacy. He brought out a small, bright, delicate metal object and asked, "What do you think this is?"

   "A small pair of pliers," someone replied.

   "Actually," the teacher said, "this is a $500 pair of fishhook removers." He held the tool in the air and pretended that he was removing a hook from a fish's mouth. "If you reach way down into the fish's mouth, you can remove the hook without damaging the fish."

   The couples were quite impressed, but then another person asked, "Why in the world would anyone pay that much money for a fishhook remover?"

   "My point exactly. Why would anyone pay that much to remove a hook from a fish's mouth?" the teacher responded. "Actually, this isn't really a fishhook remover. It's a delicate 'needle holder' used in brain surgery to hold a suture. This tool holds a suture so fine that it's hardly visible to the human eye. The neurosurgeon uses this surgical instrument under a powerful microscope during surgery. This instrument is so carefully balanced that it doesn't make the surgeon's hand tired when he sews brain tissue for long periods of time. And because of its special design and its $500 price tag, the instrument is handled carefully throughout the hospital. When used in the proper environment—the operating room—it's a wonderful tool.

   "Now," the teacher continued, "can this valuable surgical instrument be used as a fishhook remover?"

   "Yes," the couples answered.

   "Is a tackle box the environment for which this finely crafted instrument was made?" the teacher asked.

   "No!" the couples exclaimed.

   "Likewise," the teacher went on, "God created sex for a

special environment—marriage. *Whenever we take sex out of the environment for which it was created, it becomes tainted and corroded, just like this fine surgical instrument would be if it were tossed into a tackle box."*

As this story illustrates, sex is wonderful. God designed it that way. The book in the Bible called the Song of Solomon reveals the physical love between a husband and wife and the beauty of their sexual relationship. God designed sex to be the ultimate physical closeness that a man and his wife can experience. No wonder it's difficult to keep our minds from becoming consumed with the subject of sex! It is something to look forward to, but to experience all of the blessings God has for you in a marriage relationship, you must wait for His perfect timing. God's plan for some men is that they do not marry so that they can be set apart in a special way as a single man in His service. But for most of us, God already has a special woman picked out to be our bride and partner for life.

Dear brothers, you are only visitors here. Since your real home is in heaven I beg you to keep away from the evil pleasures of this world; they are not for you, for they wage war against your very soul.

1 Peter 2:11 (TLB)

1. Read 2 Corinthians 10:3-5. How can we win the battle for purity in our minds and hearts?

    _____

    _____

    _____

2a. Read Romans 6:12-13. What does God say we should not do with our bodies?

    _____

2b. What does He say we should do with our bodies?

    _____

    _____

Just as Scandalon tempted Teknon, your enemy—Satan—wants to tempt you to fail in the area of sexual purity. If he can destroy your character, you are no longer a threat to him. Satan often uses sex to tempt us to sin. He sets traps for us and, if we don't allow God to control our desires, we'll walk right into them.

3. What does the Bible say about temptation in 1 Corinthians 10:13? How much can we depend on God when we are tempted?

_____

_____

God promises to provide a way out during any temptation we face. It may mean that we shouldn't take the second look. It will probably mean getting out of the tempting situation as quickly as possible. Remember, God promises to provide the power for you to live a pure life.

THE WEDDING KISS

Now, think about the Wedding Kiss. It's a pretty radical idea, right? But why not take every precaution possible to make sure that you will have the most fulfilling and intimate life possible with the wife God may eventually bring into your life? The world's approach to sex is not about creating more exciting and satisfying relationships, although the movie and music industry would try to tell us otherwise. Sure the Wedding Kiss challenge sounds weird in today's society, but it's worth waiting for the benefits you'll receive in the long run. Besides, God is the one who designed sex; let's try it His way! Kratos said that he wished someone had challenged him to meet such a goal. There are probably many men today who wish they had received a challenge like this when they were your age.

4a. Read 1 Thessalonians 4:1-5. How do the Gentiles (non-Christians) behave regarding sexual activity?

_____

_____

It's hard to beat a person who never gives up.

Babe Ruth

4b. How does God say He wants you to behave in this area?

_____

The idea of the Wedding Kiss is not just a trendy fad to consider for a while and then move on to something else. It is a brave and bold commitment to purity. It's holding on to the precious gift of your body and emotions until you can give that gift to one special person. People who choose to refrain from sexual intimacy before marriage will be blessed by God in powerful ways.

5. What do you think your friends would think about the idea of the Wedding Kiss? How far do you think most teens will go physically with a girl?

_____

_____

6. Whether you go for the Wedding Kiss or not, you need to decide in advance how far you will go emotionally and physically with a girl before you are married. Have you ever really thought about how far you plan to go?

_____

You may have already taken a few steps toward the cliff that Kratos talked about. You may have kissed a girl, or maybe become even more physically and emotionally involved with her. If you have, now is the time to confess this to God and seek His forgiveness. Then, recommit yourself to a higher standard. Claim God's promise of forgiveness and cleansing (1 John 1:9), and start fresh today in this area of purity.

Optional Question

7. What would you have said and done if you were Teknon when Lana surprised him behind the bushes?

_____

The Main Things I learned in this Champion Session are:

_____

_____

_____

_____

_____

_____

Walk by the Spirit, and you will not carry out the desire of the flesh.

Galatians 5:16b

CHAMPION
SHEET OF DEEDS

Go to the CHAMPION Sheet of Deeds on page 9 and write down **one thing you will begin to do** before the next session (and beyond) to apply the main things you learned in session 3.

Your Mission

Complete your mission and CHAMPION Session prep before you meet for session 4.

Power Verse: 1 Corinthians 6:18

Date memorized: _____

Critical Maneuver

This will reinforce what you learned in this session. Obtain your maneuver instructions from your father.

CHAMPION Sheet of Deeds

Begin to apply your action point from your Sheet of Deeds.

CHAMPION Session Prep

Reread episode 4 of *Teknon and the CHAMPION Warriors*, and then complete the questions in session 4 in your *Mission Guide* on your own. **Our next CHAMPION Session will be:**

DATE:

_____

TIME:

_____

PLACE:

_____

Courage • Honor • Attitude • Mental toughness • Purity • Integrity • Ownership • Navigation

Session 4:
The Company I Keep

CHAMPION Characteristics
Mental Toughness and Integrity

POWER VERSE: 1 Corinthians 15:33

Do not be misled: "Bad company corrupts good character." (NIV)

Discussion Topics

Recognizing the importance of discernment in choosing friends
Realizing that there are always consequences to our choices
Recovering from failures—part 1

Mission Debrief

1. Discuss your mission from session 3. Are you taking the responsibility to complete and learn from your critical maneuvers?

   _____

2. Are you continuing to apply your action points from the Sheet of Deeds? If so, how is it going? If not, what would help you to start applying your action points?

   _____

3. Recite your power verse (1 Corinthians 6:18) from session 3.

4. Are you struggling with any sexual desires that could lead to temptation? If so, what can you do to deal with those desires (the CHAMPION's Ring)? What strength and protection do you need to gain from the Lord (God's Ring)?

   _____

   _____

5. Try to recite at least half of the CHAMPION Warrior Creed from memory (see page 5).

   _____

   _____

◆ Teknon and the CHAMPION Warriors ◆

Reconnaissance

1. Review the Map of the Mission on page 8 and determine the team's location in episode 4.

2. What is the CHAMPION definition of **Mental Toughness**? Of **Integrity**? (Refer to the CHAMPION Code on page 6.)

_____

_____

_____

_____

_____

It's not whether you get knocked down, it's whether you get up.

Vince Lombardi

3a. Do you believe Teknon used good judgment in Bia? Why or why not?

_____

_____

3b. If not, at which moments in this episode did he show a lack of discernment?

_____

_____

_____

4. When should Teknon have realized that he should avoid the Harpax?

_____

_____

5. The leader of the Harpax is named Rhegma. The Greek word *rhegma* means "ruin." In what ways could a person like Rhegma ruin the life of a young man who would join the Harpax group

_____

_____

_____

There's a story about a zoo that had a lion pavilion. One day, a visitor to the zoo was astonished as he looked in the lion cage and saw a lamb and a lion lying down together. The man couldn't believe that the natural enemies lived so peacefully together. He grabbed the zookeeper by the arm and asked him how such a wonderful relationship could occur. The zookeeper replied, "It's easy, Mister, we just add fresh lambs now and then."

When you make friends with the wrong people, like Teknon did with the Harpax, you can end up in trouble. Bottom line: be careful whom you trust and to whom you offer friendship.

OPTIONAL QUESTION

6. Why do you think Kratos allowed Teknon to meet with the Harpax?

_____

_____

7. What did Kratos mean when he said, "It's better to be trusted and respected than it is to be liked"?

_____

_____

8. Kratos also told Teknon that he must learn from his mistake and to recover. What does it mean to recover? How would you recover if you made a mistake like Teknon made?

_____

_____

Optional Questions

9. Kratos cautioned, "Observe all of the characteristics of a person." What characteristics should you watch for?

GOOD Characteristics:

_____

_____

BAD Characteristics:

_____

_____

10. What do you think Kratos meant when he said, "Bad humor is a sign of bad morals"?

_____

_____

Hold yourself responsible for a higher standard than anybody else expects of you. Never excuse yourself.

Henry Ward Beecher

STRATEGY AND TACTICS

We need friends that not only make us feel good, but also cause us to do good things. Because of this, it is important to seek God's wisdom as you develop friendships.

Most of the book of Proverbs in the Old Testament was written by one of the wisest men who ever lived, King Solomon. In this book, Solomon instructed his sons and the young men of his kingdom about the difference between knowledge (having the facts) and wisdom (applying those facts to life). Like Teknon, young men can choose to reject the wisdom of their parents and the Word of God. As they grow older, however, they will increase their knowledge, but not their wisdom and discernment. In Proverbs 1, Solomon described the danger of being a young man who lacks discernment.

1a. Read Proverbs 1. What can a person do to begin obtaining wisdom? (See verses 7-9.)

_____

Rather fail with honor than succeed by fraud.

Sophocles

1b. What advice did Solomon give in verses 15 and 16 concerning the importance of choosing the right friends?

_____

_____

1c. According to verses 23-27, why should we listen to sound advice and wisdom?

_____

1d. What will happen if we don't obey God and use discernment? (See verses 28-32.)

_____

_____

1e. What will happen if we use good judgment and listen to wisdom? (See verse 33.)

_____

_____

Always remember two things about your Heavenly Father: God loves you and He is trustworthy.

God loves you

Just as Kratos loved Teknon despite his bad decisions, so your Father in heaven loves you no matter what you do. He understands that you are growing and learning how to follow Him. Sometimes you will succeed, and sometimes you will fail. As you grow to know Him better and seek to obey His Word, you will increase in discernment and find it easier to make better choices.

But no matter how hard we try, we will still sin and disobey God. Romans 3:23 tells us that we have all sinned. God understands us and loves us so much that He sent Jesus to die on the cross and then raised Him again from the dead to pay for our sins (or failures). After we sin, we recover by confessing our failure to God and then claiming His promise of forgiveness. Then, we turn from our own way and go God's way. We should also apologize to anyone we have offended.

2. What does 1 John 1:9 say about God and confessing our sins to Him? How does this make you feel?

_____

_____

Associate yourself with men of good quality if you esteem your own reputation; for it is better to be alone than in bad company.

George Washington

God is trustworthy

God is trustworthy and all-knowing. If you need wisdom, you can trust Him to provide it for you. All you have to do is ask.

"If you want to know what God wants you to do, ask Him, and He will gladly tell you, for He is always ready to give a bountiful supply of wisdom to all who ask Him; He will not resent it." (James 1:5 TLB)

3. In what ways can God give you answers about choosing friends and other issues?

_____

_____

4. Why is belief in who God is so important?

_____

As a future CHAMPION, you must remember to ask for wisdom before you enter situations like those Teknon faced in the city of Bia. In other words, use good judgment ahead of time and study how God wants you to respond before you enter a tempting situation.

Optional Questions

5. Kratos used the Hoplon to become invisible. What would you do if you could become invisible?

_____

6. What kind of friend will help you to do good as well as to feel good? What are the characteristics of such a person?

_____

7. Why did George Washington say, "It's better to be alone than in bad company"?

_____

_____

The Main Things I learned in this Champion Session are:

_____

_____

_____

_____

CHAMPION
Sheet of Deeds

Go to the CHAMPION Sheet of Deeds on page 9 and write down **one thing you will begin to do** in before the next session (and beyond) to apply the main things you learned in session 4.

Your Mission

Complete your mission and CHAMPION Session prep before you meet for Session 5.

Power Verse: 1 Corinthians 15:33

Date memorized: _____

Critical Maneuver

This will reinforce what you learned today. Obtain your maneuver instructions from your father.

CHAMPION Sheet of Deeds

Begin to apply your action point from your Sheet of Deeds.

CHAMPION Session Prep

Reread episode 5 of *Teknon and the CHAMPION Warriors*, and then complete the questions in session 5 in your *Mission Guide* on your own. **Our next CHAMPION Session will be:**

DATE:

_____

TIME:

_____

PLACE:

_____

He who walks with wise men will be wise, but the companion of fools will suffer harm.

Proverbs 13:20

Courage • Honor • Attitude • Mental toughness • Purity • Integrity • Ownership • Navigation

Session 5:
Ergonian Pride

CHAMPION Characteristic
Attitude

POWER VERSE: PROVERBS 19:20 (NIV)

Listen to advice and accept instruction, and in the end you will be wise.

Discussion Topics

Uncovering the danger of pride
Learning the importance of a teachable attitude
Listening to wise counsel

Mission Debrief

1. Discuss your mission from session 4. What did you learn from your maneuver? How is what you learned affecting your thinking or behavior?

   _____

   _____

   _____

2. Did you start applying your new action point from the Sheet of Deeds? If so, how is it going?

   _____

   _____

   _____

3. Recite your power verse (1 Corinthians 15:33) from session 4.

4a. If you are spending time with people who influence you in bad ways, what steps should you take to change that situation? (Remember, the CHAMPION's Ring from session 1 contains those areas that you can and should control.)

   _____

   _____

4b. Are you worried about any other people's perception of you? Is it difficult for you to trust God with those perceptions and your concerns? If so, why do you think that is? (This is part of God's Ring, the area that only He can control and that we need to release to Him.)

_____

_____

5. Try to recite all of the CHAMPION Warrior Creed from memory (see page 5).

Reconnaissance

1. Review the Map of the Mission on page 8 and determine the team's location in episode 5. Trace the steps the team has covered thus far, reviewing story highlights and main topics discussed.

_____

_____

_____

2. What is the CHAMPION definition of **Attitude**? (Refer to the CHAMPION Code on page 6.)

_____

_____

_____

_____

3. What kind of attitude did Mr. Poroo have toward Kratos? Why?

_____

_____

4. Why did Kratos say, "That attitude might be his undoing"?

_____

_____

When a man is wrapped up in himself, he makes a pretty small package.

John Ruskin

5. What occurred as a result of Mr. Poroo's attitude?

_____

_____

6. In what ways might Mr. Poroo have responded differently to Kratos' suggestion? How would the outcome have been different ?

_____

_____

7. What does the word "teachability" mean to you? Be specific!

_____

_____

Gleukos was the socially acceptable intoxicant consumed by the resort guests at Ergo. Kratos explained why the guests used this substance: "This is a place to escape. For a few days, all these people want to do is to forget about their lives at home. Sun, fun, eating, and drinking gleukos is what this place is all about."

✦ Teknon and the CHAMPION Warriors ✦

8. What do you think about teens drinking alcohol? What about adults?

Strategy and Tactics

Easy Mistakes

Have you ever acted like you knew it all? We all have. Let's say you're facing an important decision, like buying a new sound system. You see one you like, but don't really know how good it is. You know your neighbor is an expert on these systems and could provide you with excellent information to help you decide which one to buy and might even know the best place to buy it. But you have your pride and don't want to reveal your lack of "surround sound, high density, bass-enriched" expertise. So you don't ask anyone for advice, especially your expert neighbor. What do you do? You buy an overpriced player that breaks down within three months. Of course, the warranty is only good for 30 days.

A few days later, you're over at a new friend's house on a rainy day. Your friend is a proud owner of a new, streamlined dirt bike. He tells you there's no better time to dirt bike than on a rainy day; in fact, the wetter the better. He tells you that if you haven't ridden a dirt bike before, he'd be more than happy to give you a quick lesson. You've never ridden anything more tenacious than a 10-speed, but that's a well-kept secret. *Nothing doing*, you say to yourself. You're not about to look "mechanically challenged" around your buddy. What do you do? You jump on, rev the engine and pop the clutch. Thirty feet of mud and a compound fracture later, you're wondering why you didn't take your friend up on his free introductory lesson.

After you get out of the hospital, your dad expresses concern about one of your new friends. He's bothered that this new acquaintance encourages you to watch dirty movies, tell lies, and use vulgar language. You immediately respond by defending the friend and declaring that your dad is intolerant and that he's overreacting. Basically you ignore the whole

The only discipline
that lasts is
self-discipline.

"Bum" Phillips

discussion. A couple months later, you're using profanity, struggling with pornography, and lying to your parents to cover it up.

Life would be much easier if we were teachable, wouldn't it?

1. What does Proverbs 19:20 say about being teachable?

_____

2. What happens if you are not teachable? (Read Proverbs 29:1.)

_____

_____

Read Proverbs 16:18-19 and Proverbs 18:12.

3a. What kind of attitude creates the greatest barrier to becoming teachable and leads to your destruction in the end?

_____

3b. What kind of attitude makes us teachable and leads to honor?

_____

_____

4. According to Psalm 50:15, who should we call on first if we need help or have a big decision to make? How will He respond?

_____

_____

If you have invited Jesus into your life as your Savior and Lord, you are a child of God. God loves it when His children call on Him.

When we seek God, we honor Him. Jeremiah 29:11-13 (TLB) says, "For I know the plans I have for you," says the Lord. "They are plans for good and not for evil, to give you a future and a hope. In those days when you pray, I will listen. You will find me when you seek me if you look for me in earnest."

God knows what is best for us. When we reject God's wisdom and direction in our decisions, we are trying to do His job. When we aren't teachable, we don't pay attention to God's Word. We also don't listen to people whom God puts into our lives to give us advice and counsel—like our parents, pastors, and teachers. We saw what happened to Mr. Poroo when he didn't listen to Kratos' advice. Make sure you are seeking God with a teachable heart so that He can reveal how to live your life for Him.

5. Do you think your friends (name a few) are teachable? Why or why not?

Read Proverbs 6:20-23

My son, observe the commandment of your father and do not forsake the teaching of your mother; bind them continually on your heart; tie them around your neck. When you walk about, they will guide you; when you sleep, they will watch over you; and when you awake, they will talk to you. For the commandment is a lamp, and the teaching is light; and reproofs for discipline are the way of life ... .

_____

_____

6a. What are the some of the benefits of listening to your parents?

_____

6b. Has this discussion changed your view about the importance of your parents' advice and discipline? How so? Do you need to adjust your attitude in this area?

_____

_____

> *Success isn't forever, and failure isn't fatal.*
>
> Don Shula

The Main Things I learned in this Champion Session are:

_____

_____

_____

_____

_____

_____

> *Teachability is a man's capacity for growth.*
>
> Howard Hendricks

CHAMPION
Sheet of Deeds

Go to the CHAMPION Sheet of Deeds on page 9 and write down **one thing you will begin to do** before the next session (and beyond) to apply the main things you learned in session 5.

Your Mission

Complete your mission and CHAMPION Session Prep before you meet for session 6.

POWER VERSE: PROVERBS 19:20

Date memorized: _____

CRITICAL MANEUVER

This will reinforce what you learned in this session. Obtain your maneuver instructions from your father.

CHAMPION SHEET OF DEEDS

Begin to apply your action point from your Sheet of Deeds.

CHAMPION SESSION PREP

Reread episode 6 of Teknon and the CHAMPION Warriors, and then complete the questions in session 6 in your Mission Guide on your own. **Our next CHAMPION Session will be:**

DATE:

_____

TIME:

_____

PLACE:

_____

Spend less time worrying who's right, and spend more time deciding what's right!

Life's Little Instruction Book

Courage • Honor • Attitude • Mental toughness • Purity • Integrity • Ownership • Navigation

Session 6:
A Storm of Dishonor

Champion Characteristics
Honor and Attitude

Power Verse: Romans 12:10

Be devoted to one another in brotherly love; give preference to one another in honor.

Discussion Topics

Showing respect to family members
Showing honor—placing value on people and
communicating that value to them

Mission Debrief

1. Discuss your mission from session 5. What did you learn from your maneuver? How is what you've learned affecting your thinking and behavior?

    _____

    _____

2. Did you start applying your new action point from the Sheet of Deeds? If so, what are you learning? If not, what would help you to get started?

    _____

    _____

3. Recite your power verse (Proverbs 19:20) from session 5.

4. Think about any area(s) of your life in which you need to be more teachable. What are they? What will you change to become more teachable? (Attitudes and actions like these, which you control, are within the CHAMPION's Ring.)

    _____

    _____

    _____

5. Try to recite all of the CHAMPION Warrior Creed from memory (see page 5). Say it slowly and think about which characteristics mean the most to you.

Reconnaissance

1. Review the Map of the Mission on page 8 and determine the team's location in episode 6.

2. What is the CHAMPION definition of **Honor**? Of **Attitude**? (Refer to the CHAMPION Code on page 6.)

_____

_____

_____

_____

3. How did Pikros and Parakoe treat their father? What did they reveal about their relationship with him?

_____

_____

4. How did Pikros and Parakoe treat each other?

_____

_____

_____

5. How did Teknon feel as he observed the boys' attitudes toward their father? Why did he feel this way?

_____

_____

⊙ptio♢al Questio♢s

6. In the Greek, *pikros* refers to acting bitterly. Pikros was disrespectful to his father and bitter about their relationship. Why do you think Pikros was bitter about the relationship with his father?

_____

7. Ameleo said, "I try to give them [my sons] everything they want." Why didn't this help Pikros and Parakoe to develop a better attitude toward their father? What did they really need and want?

_____

_____

_____

_____

Kind words do not cost much ... yet they accomplish much.

Blaise Pascal

8. What did Kratos mean when he said, "No matter what we accomplish or who we impress, if we don't treat our family and friends with respect, we have nothing to offer"?

_____

_____

_____

9. How did watching Pikros and Parakoe affect Teknon's attitude toward his sister Hilly?

_____

_____

_____

10. Do you think Teknon shows respect toward his father and mother? Why do you think so?

_____

_____

_____

The deepest principle in human nature is the craving to be appreciated.

William James

STRATEGY AND TACTICS

Honor and respect seem to be lost virtues in our society. We suffer from what has been called "a toxic atmosphere of cynicism" throughout the schools and boardrooms of our country. A newspaper article entitled "Nasty as We Wanna Be" lamented our current attitudes by stating that:

> *The old values of courtesy, politeness, and respect have been trampled under. We, as men, need to communicate to our sons what it means to show respect and esteem to the individuals God brings into our lives. The indignities of the road are compounded with further indignities at work, at the movies, on the radio, from the profane mouths of strangers, and in battles between neighbors. Pretty soon, you've got more than a headache. You've got a crisis on your hands.*
>
> *If we, as Christians, don't lead the way toward honoring people and treating them with dignity as individuals created by God, who will?[1]*

An Honorable Attitude

Read Exodus 20:12. This is one of the Ten Commandments.

1a. What does this commandment say about the attitude young people should have toward their parents?

_____

1b. What does God promise the results will be if we obey His commandment?

_____

_____

2. What are some practical ways in which you can show honor to your parents? (Remember the CHAMPION's Ring involves your attitude and behavior.)

_____

_____

_____

Most of us, swimming against the tides of trouble the world knows nothing about, need only a bit of praise or encouragement— and we'll make the goal.

Jerome P. Fleishman

3. What does Galatians 6:9-10 say about how young people should treat their brothers and sisters?

_____

_____

_____

_____

_____

◆ TEKNON AND THE CHAMPION WARRIORS ◆

4. Read Romans 12:10. How can we "do good" within our family?

_____

_____

_____

_____

The Bible says we ought to "do good to all people." That should especially apply to our family members.

5. How do you view your parents? How about your brothers and sisters? Do you act like Pikros and Parakoe? Or do you view your family, even with their flaws, as valuable people given to you by God?

_____

_____

The members of your family are valuable gifts that God has given you. Are they always easy to get along with? No way! Are you?

Does what they do always make sense? Absolutely not! Does what you do always make sense? Enough said.

A CHAMPION strives to maintain the right attitudes, no matter what other people do. Read Genesis 37:18-36. Joseph's brothers sold him into slavery because they were jealous of him. Even though his capture was a terrible thing, God used Joseph's captivity in an awesome way to eventually place Joseph as the second most powerful man in the Egyptian empire.

Read Genesis 45 to see how Joseph forgave his brothers even when he had the power to hurt them. Joseph understood that "God causes all things to work together for good to those who love God, to those who are called according to His purpose" (see Romans 8:28b).

6a. If your brother or sister doesn't show you honor, what should you do?

_____

_____

_____

6b. Why should you respond this way?

_____

_____

_____

Remember the three R's: Respect for self, Respect for others, and Responsibility for your actions.

Life's Little Instruction Book II

You should honor your parents as God's chosen authority in your life. If you have any brothers and sisters, you should honor them as treasured co-workers and help your family to become all that God wants it to be. Don't end up like Pikros and Parakoe. Remember, you honor God by the way you treat other people. Take steps as a CHAMPION to maintain the right *Attitude* and show *Honor* to your family.

7. What are some practical ways you can you show honor to your mother? How about your brothers and sisters?

_____

_____

_____

_____

The Main Things I learned in this Champion Session are:

_____

_____

_____

_____

_____

A man's wisdom gives him patience; it is to his glory to overlook an offense.

Proverbs 19:11 (NIV)

CHAMPION
Sheet of Deeds

Go to the CHAMPION Sheet of Deeds on page 9 and write down **one thing you will begin to do** before the next session (and beyond) to apply the main things you learned in session 6.

Your Mission

Complete your mission and CHAMPION Session Prep before you meet for session 7.

Power Verse: Romans 12:10

Date memorized: _____

Critical Maneuver

This will reinforce what you learned in this session. Obtain your maneuver instructions from your father.

CHAMPION Sheet of Deeds

Begin to apply your action point from your Sheet of Deeds.

CHAMPION Session Prep

Reread episode 7 of *Teknon and the CHAMPION Warriors*, and then complete the questions in session 7 in your *Mission Guide* on your own. **Our next CHAMPION Session will be:**

DATE:

_____

TIME:

_____

PLACE:

_____

Courage • Honor • Attitude • Mental toughness • Purity • Integrity • Ownership • Navigation

Session 7:
An Excellent Choice

CHAMPION Characteristics
Purity and Integrity

POWER VERSE: PSALM 101:3

I will set no worthless thing before my eyes; I hate the work [deeds] of those who fall away; it shall not fasten its grip on me.

Discussion Topics

Protecting your mind from inappropriate material
Avoiding temptation
Fleeing from temptation
Establishing your convictions in advance

Mission Debrief

1. Discuss your mission from session 6. What did you learn from your maneuver? How is this affecting your attitude or behavior?

   _____

   _____

2. Did you start applying your new action point from the Sheet of Deeds? What are some of the things you're learning from this and the previous action points?

   _____

   _____

3. Recite your power verse (Romans 12:10) from session 6.

4. Describe one situation when you honored your mother and/or father since the last CHAMPION Session? Describe one way you have honored your brothers/sisters or other family members? (Remember that honoring others is part of the actions and attitudes in the CHAMPION's Ring.)

   _____

   _____

5. Recite all of the CHAMPION Warrior Creed from memory (see page 5).

Reconnaissance

1. Review the Map of the Mission on page 8 before beginning this section. Identify where the team is located in episode 7.

2. Review the CHAMPION definition of **Purity** and of **Integrity** (refer to the CHAMPION Code on page 6.)

_____

_____

_____

_____

3. *Epios* is a Greek word that refers to someone who shows patience and gentleness to other people. What does Epios (Epps) do to live up to his name?

_____

_____

4. What did Eros try to get Teknon to do? Why?

_____

_____

_____

5. Why do you think Teknon chose not to stay in the image salon and look at the images?

_____

_____

_____

6. Why do you think Kratos said that looking at pictures of nude women gives a distorted view of women, love, and sex?

_____

_____

_____

7. Why were Kratos and the mentors so excited about Teknon's decision to leave the imaging salon?

_____

_____

_____

8. Even though Teknon made an excellent choice at the imaging salon, when did he make a bad choice?

_____

_____

_____

_____

Epps helped Teknon to see the danger that surrounded him when he said, "You [Teknon] took a big chance when you decided to go out on your own and walk past those places. All of us are tempted to look at bad material like that, but we can't afford to take those kinds of risks. We've got to stay as far away from them as possible."

STRATEGY AND TACTICS

DON'T PET THE T-REX!

Several years ago, my daughter and I went on a lunch date. After enjoying a great meal in the restaurant, we decided to walk through some nearby stores.

As soon as we entered a pet store named Fishes of the World, we knew that we had discovered a great place to explore. Exotic pets from around the world filled its cages and aquariums. We were surrounded by eels, fish, spiders, and snakes. One glass case was filled with very cute lizards—that's right, cute lizards. They were about five inches long and had big, friendly eyes—almost like a Labrador Retriever. Just take my word for it: they were cute.

When the store's owner saw us pausing to look at the lizards, he took one out for us to hold. It snuggled in my hand and almost purred as my daughter and I petted it. "What's the name of this type of lizard? I asked.

"It's a Savannah Monitor," the owner said.

"Is this as big as it gets?" I asked, still petting the calm lizard.

"Oh, no," he responded. "In fact, there's a grown Savannah over there." We followed him around the corner to a much larger cage encased with thick wire. Inside was a reptile about four feet long that looked like it was on loan from the movie "Lost World." When my daughter and I stepped closer, the big lizard whipped around and snapped at the front of the cage.

"Yep," said the owner, "you can walk one around on a leash when it gets this size, but it'll drag you around a bit. You'd have to close in your backyard, of course." Then he added, "I wouldn't let children walk back there, though."

I found it hard to believe that the little, purring reptile I'd held in my hand a few minutes earlier could one day look at my children the way I look at a cheese pizza!

Bad habits are a lot like that cute little lizard. At first a bad habit seems harmless, and we don't believe there is any way it could hurt us. We get comfortable with it, feed it, and soon it begins to grow. Before long, it consumes more time and effort than before. In fact, the habit can become so strong that it is difficult to control. *Soon, it gets so powerful that it can start to control us and drag us around.*

Viewing pornography—sexually explicit material—is one of the most dangerous habits you can develop. It can be compared to petting a baby T-Rex and bringing it into your home. Why in the world would you want to pet a T-Rex *or* bring it into your home? You could never tame it, and you sure couldn't control it.

1. What are some of the sources of pornography in our society? (Hint: Think about what you see and hear.)

   _____

   _____

   _____

2. What do you think pornography does to a person's mind?

   _____

   _____

   _____

   _____

   _____

◆ Teknon and the Champion Warriors ◆

Our minds act like computers and also like cameras. Just as a computer's response is based on the data programmed into it, whatever data we put into our minds will affect how we view the world and how we respond to it. It's not quite this simple because our minds are far more complex than any computer in the world, but the basic principles work the same way.

You have probably heard the phrase, "garbage in, garbage out." When we allow ourselves to view sexually explicit material, it's like downloading a computer virus into the hard-drive of our minds. Those images start to corrupt our thinking and how we react to other people.

Our minds are also like a camera because, when we look at a pornographic picture or movie, our minds record it—and store it to be brought back again and again.

3a. What does Romans 12:2 mean by "do not be conformed to this world"?

_____

_____

3b. What do you think "renewing of your mind" means?

_____

_____

_____

_____

As we choose to draw near to God and yield our lives to the power of His Holy Spirit, He will give us the power NOT to conform to this world. As we allow God to reshape our defective thinking to align with His mind, our attitudes and actions will change. Life-change occurs from the inside out.

4. What do you think this phrase means: "let us throw off everything that hinders and the sin that so easily entangles" (Hebrews 12:1b NIV)?

_____

_____

_____

Do not offer the parts of your body to sin, as instruments of wickedness, but rather offer yourselves to God, as those who have been brought from death to life; and offer the parts of your body to Him as instruments of righteousness.

Romans 6:13 (NIV)

Embracing temptation and viewing pornography is sin. Like other sins, it will weigh us down in every aspect of our lives. Did you know that pornography could easily become addicting, just like drinking alcohol or snorting cocaine? Addictions can kill you spiritually, mentally, and physically. The best way to avoid becoming addicted to something dangerous like pornography is to stay away from it altogether.

But that's not easy is it? Pornography is easily available today. Suddenly an ad comes on TV with a sexy woman wearing little of anything. Some of your friends bring a picture or magazine to school and ask you to look at it. You visit someone's house, only to find out that they plan to watch an 'R' rated movie that includes sexual scenes. Maybe a friend wants to show you a sex site on the Web.

5a. What would you do if something like this happened to you?

_____

_____

5b. Have any kids at school brought dirty pictures to school? Do any of them talk about seeing naked women on the Internet? What do you do when they say that?"

_____

_____

_____

6. According to Psalm 101:3, what should your stand be on pornography or any explicit images that tempt you?

_____

7. What does God promise to offer you if you are willing to trust Him when you face a temptation (read 1 Corinthians 10:13)?

_____

_____

_____

Hoplon is a Greek term that refers to armor or weapons of warfare. Just as Teknon and Kratos need their armor to protect them in the battle, Christians also need armor—spiritual armor. The Bible describes this armor of God in Ephesians 6:10-18.

8. What makes up the spiritual armor that God provides for us ? How could this armor help you to gain more self-discipline in what you watch, listen to, and read?

_____

_____

_____

_____

_____

_____

These physical objects are metaphors representing God's gifts of protection and spiritual weapons that will help us in the battle against temptation. We need to put on God's full armor or we will not be ready to do battle with Satan. We must trust God and make the right choices in what we see, think, and do.

When you put on the armor of God, it's almost like Kratos putting on the Hoplon. God gives you all of the weapons you need to fight your enemy, Satan. Satan would like nothing more than for you to start a habit of looking at the pornographic or sensual material so that your relationship with God and other people would be hindered.

Failure to prepare is preparing to fail.

John Wooden

9. What do you think are some of the benefits of not looking at pornography?

_____

_____

_____

Let's get practical. Here are some suggestions that will help you gain control over this area of your mind, now and in the future. But, to gain control of your mind, you have to make the right choices, even when you're alone.

Movies. Set a standard for what movie rating levels you will not watch. Using the movie rating standards is tough because some "R" rated films are not as bad as some of those rated "PG-13" or even "PG". But, remember, a film that carries a "PG-13" or "R" rating does so for a reason. You can save yourself a lot of headaches and uncomfortable situations with your friends, by telling them you have decided to stay away from these ratings. You can and should check with your father about which movies are acceptable to watch. The real standard you need, God's standard, is found in Philippians 4:8.

Dwell or think only on things that meet God's standard—the PHIL 4:8 standard:

Whatever is:

- true
- honorable
- right
- pure
- lovely
- admirable
- excellent
- worthy of praise

DVD's and Videos. The same suggestions apply here. This category is far more available and will require integrity on your part, especially when you are at a friend's house and his parents are gone.

Magazines. Obviously, you need to avoid pornographic magazines like the plague. But, you also need to be careful of publications that are not openly focused on sex, yet talk a lot about it. Reading these magazines and looking at the pictures can entice you to look at something worse. Remember the Shocktech problem—"Error increases with distance."

Cable Television. With more channels comes more opportunity to watch the wrong stuff. Plan ahead of time, which shows you will watch, and which ones you won't. Channel surfing is a dangerous sport; don't play it!

Internet. Every computer needs neon signs around it that flash, "Beware, hazardous roads ahead!" Before you start 'surfing' on the 'Super Highway', do yourself a favor and have your parents set the controls to prevent entry to the bad sites. Be purposeful. Decide which information you need, get it, and get out. The Internet has already ruined many men's minds because of careless surfing. And be careful of chat rooms. Even chat rooms geared toward young people can take off in a sexual direction without advance notice.

Music. What you hear can influence you as much as what you watch. Stay away from music that describes sexual intimacy and violence. And don't let yourself get drawn into the trap of watching music videos on cable channels.

Video Games. Whether at home or at the arcade, video games are becoming more violent and more sexually suggestive. Don't let yourself get sucked into the never-ending spiral of destructive competition that these games offer.

Setting high standards for what you watch, read, and listen to is a lot like racing toward that cliff Kratos described a few episodes ago. The best time to put on the brakes is when you know the cliff *is* ahead. The danger from pornography, like the cliff, is ahead. Remember your part in the CHAMPION Ring and take the responsibility to set high standards. Decide to put on your brakes now by refusing to look at any pornography. Also trust God to give you the strength to turn away from this material and to encircle you with his ring of protection even before the pictures or words cross your path. Ask your father or mother, and one of your trusted Christian friends, to pray for you and make sure you are holding the line in this area.

Take heart if you have already failed or even developed a bad habit in this area. Remember that God loves you and is waiting for you to seek His forgiveness. Don't let the guilt that so often comes with this habit overtake you and make you depressed. You can restore fellowship with God today and draw on His strength to help you kick the habit. Jesus said, "I have overcome the world" (John 16:33). Since He has overcome the world, He can help you overcome your habits and tendencies. Be courageous enough to share your difficulties with your father today and ask him to help you.

Don't pet the T-Rex of pornography. At first, it may purr like a kitten, but sooner or later it will bite like a Savannah Monitor.

> *I do not pray for success. I ask for faithfulness.*
>
> Mother Teresa

THE MAIN THINGS I LEARNED IN THIS CHAMPION SESSION ARE:

_____

_____

_____

_____

CHAMPION
SHEET OF DEEDS

Go to the CHAMPION Sheet of Deeds on page 9 and write down **one thing you will begin to do** before the next session (and beyond) to apply the main things you learned in session 7.

Your Mission

Complete your mission and CHAMPION Session Prep before you meet for session 8.

POWER VERSE: PSALM 101:3

Date memorized: _____

CRITICAL MANEUVER

This will reinforce what you learned in this session. Obtain your maneuver instructions from your father.

CHAMPION SHEET OF DEEDS

Begin to apply your action point from your Sheet of Deeds.

CHAMPION Session Prep

Reread episode 8 of *Teknon and the CHAMPION Warriors*, and then complete the questions in session 8 in your *Mission Guide* on your own. **Our next CHAMPION Session will be:**

DATE:

_____

TIME:

_____

PLACE:

_____

Special Topic Note Pages

Session 8:
Faced With Fear

Champion Characteristic

Courage

Power Verse: Joshua 1:9 (NIV)

Have I not commanded you? Be strong and courageous. Do not be terrified; do not be discouraged, for the Lord your God will be with you wherever you go.

Discussion Topics

Overcoming fear of rejection and fear of failure
Learning to recover from failure—part 2

Mission Debrief

1. Discuss your mission from session 7. What did you learn from your maneuver? How is what you've learned affecting your attitude or behavior?

_____

2. How will you continue to apply all of your action points from the Sheet of Deeds thus far? The goal for these is to see some habit patterns changing in your life. Are any changes occurring as you continue to apply all your various actions points?

_____

_____

3. Recite your power verse (Psalm 101:3) from session 7.

4a. Have you been more aware of areas where you need to be more careful in what you set before your eyes or hear with your ears? What are you doing to protect yourself in the following areas? (Exercise your responsibility within the CHAMPION's Ring.)

- ■ Movies
- ■ The Internet
- ■ Video games
- ■ Television
- ■ Music
- ■ Magazines

4b. When you are faced with an opportunity to look at pornography, what will you do to gain God's strength to resist that temptation? (What's in God's Ring?)

_____

_____

5. Recite the CHAMPION Warrior Creed. Say it as you would to a group of people; speak slowly and clearly.

Reconnaissance

1. Review the Map of the Mission on page 8 and determine the team's location in episode 8.

2. Review the CHAMPION definition of **Courage**. (Refer to the CHAMPION Code on page 6.)

_____

_____

3. What happened to Teknon during the team's fight with the footsoldiers?

_____

_____

4. Why do you think Teknon responded the way he did during the battle?

_____

_____

The credit belongs to the man who is actually in the arena; whose face is marred by dust and sweat and blood; who strives valiantly; who errs and comes up short again and again; who knows the great enthusiasms, the great devotions, and spends himself in a worthy cause; who at the best knows in the end the triumph of high achievement; and who at the worst, if he fails, at least fails while daring greatly ...

Theodore Roosevelt

5. How did Teknon feel about his performance during the battle? Why?

_____

_____

6. How did the footsoldier manage to hurt Kratos?

_____

Optional Questions

7. Could Kratos have prevented getting injured by the footsoldier? If so, how?

_____

8. The CHAMPION Warriors worked well as a team. When you face problems, why is teamwork so important?

_____

_____

---

9. What did Epps mean when he said, "It takes time to learn how to respond correctly in battle."?

_____

_____

10. Epps also coached Teknon that, "You learn by doing." How does this apply to Teknon?

_____

_____

Strategy and Tactics

The size of a person is determined by what it takes to stop him.

Dr. Howard Hendricks

Failure is an essential part of life. It can also be an expensive part of life. At the end of the movie "Apollo 13," actor Tom Hanks quotes his character, astronaut Jim Lovell with this statement: "They called Apollo 13 a successful failure. We didn't make it to the moon, but we returned safely."

Gene Krantz, mission control specialist of Apollo 13, vented his frustration at two other NASA officials after hearing them discuss the potential, impending disaster to the space program after this setback. "Excuse me gentlemen," he barked. "I believe this will be our finest hour."

Failure has two faces. There are *successful* failures, and there are *unsuccessful* failures. Apollo 13 was a successful failure. Not only did the astronauts return home safely under incredibly difficult circumstances, they also exercised a high level of creative output and genuine teamwork over a period of only five days that rivals any single human endeavor of the century.

Learning to Recover

Dave Simmons, former linebacker of the Dallas Cowboys, had an interesting football philosophy that applies to the rest of life too. He said, "Every play is a game; learn to recover, recover, recover."

Simmons explained in his seminar *Dad the Family Shepherd* that every play during a football game is like a game in itself. The team plans for the play, gets information for the play, and then executes the play. Usually the play is a success. Sometimes it's not. Whether or not the play is successful, the team must come back and execute again.

Let's say it's second down and ten yards to go. The quarterback throws a short pass over the middle. His eyes widen because it's almost intercepted. If it had been intercepted, the cornerback on the other team would have run for a touchdown. After the play, the quarterback is back in the huddle. What is he going to think? What is he going to do?

*In great attempts,
it is glorious
even to fail.*

Vince Lombardi

The quarterback has to do three things. (1) He must learn from his mistake of throwing the ball late. (2) He must decide what he is going to do on the next play. (3) He must recover from the mistake and move on to the next play! The more he plays, the less he will make that mistake again. What would happen if he said to himself, *Gosh, I shouldn't have thrown that pass; it was almost intercepted. I guess I just shouldn't play football.* Nonsense!

There are times when failure is a natural consequence of living. In fact, God often uses trials and failures as a learning process in our lives. When He does this, we learn, as Epps said, by doing. In James 1:2-4 the NIV Bible tells us, "Consider it pure joy, my brothers, when you face trials of many kinds, because you know that the testing of your faith develops perseverance. Perseverance must finish its work so that you may be mature and complete, not lacking anything."

There are times, however, when we fail because we run from responsibility. Sometimes we run because we aren't prepared for the challenge we face. Sometimes we run because we fear the criticism we might receive from our peers as a result of taking the responsibility. And sometimes we run because we fear the possibility of failure.

Failure, Forgiveness, and Fortification

Failure can have another name—sin. Sin, simply put, is falling short of God's perfect standard, which results in broken fellowship with Him. Whether we sin by active disobedience or rebellion, or by passive indifference, the result is the same. But we can recover from this type of failure and make it successful.

When we avoid responsibility, we must get back into the game as soon as possible. The recovery progresses in three stages:

I. **Failure**: We make the wrong decision, do the wrong thing, or find ourselves unable to succeed in a task.

II. **Forgiveness**: If sin is involved, we seek to restore fellowship with God by asking His forgiveness for our mistake. Then we forgive ourselves for our poor choice and weakness. We also seek forgiveness from people we have hurt.

III. **Fortification**: We recognize God's forgiveness for our failure and His grace for our limitations, learn from our mistakes, and try again.

If we confess our sins, He [God] is faithful and righteous to forgive us our sins and to cleanse us from all unrighteousness.

1 John 1:9

✦ Teknon and the Champion Warriors ✦

The Bible describes how the apostle Peter recovered after failing Jesus several times.

1. Check out Matthew 16:21-23. How did Peter respond toward Jesus and his prediction of his own suffering and death? How did Jesus respond to Peter?

_____

_____

_____

_____

2a. According to Luke 22:54-62, what did Peter do when Jesus was on the verge of being crucified?

_____

_____

2b. What do you think Peter's responsibility was to Jesus in this situation?

_____

_____

2c. Why do you think Peter ran from responsibility and failed Jesus in His time of need?

_____

_____

_____

3. Read John 21:15-19 and Acts 2:38-47. Was Peter able to recover from his failures to obey and follow Christ? How do you know?

_____

_____

_____

Peter was one of Jesus' closest friends. In fact, Jesus referred to Peter as the "Rock" because of his faith and strength of character. When Jesus told Peter that all of His friends would eventually deny him, Peter promised that he would never do such a thing. And yet, Peter ran from his responsibility on the night Jesus was crucified. When asked about his friendship with Christ, Peter denied that he even knew Jesus three times!

"What a cowardly failure Peter was!" we might say. How could he recover from such a mistake? Well, he not only sought forgiveness from God for his mistake, but he went on to become one of the most powerful preachers the world has ever known. Peter recovered!

4. Have you ever felt like a failure the way Teknon felt after the battle? Do you think God understands that you aren't perfect?

_____

_____

5. Read Psalm 103:13-14 and 1 Corinthians 1:25-27. What do these verses teach us about our own strength and God's understanding of how we're put together?

_____

_____

_____

Even though large tracts of Europe have fallen or may fall into the grip of the Gestapo and all the odious apparatus of Nazi rule, we shall not flag nor fail. We shall go on to the end, we shall fight in France, we shall fight on the seas and the oceans, we shall fight with growing confidence and growing strength in the air, we shall defend our island, whatever the cost may be ... we shall never surrender.

Winston Churchill (before Parliament in June 1940)

God knows that we make mistakes. He knows us better than we know ourselves because He created us. If you've made a mistake you can recover. If you've run from responsibility, you can recover. If you've been criticized, you can recover. God has unlimited power to enable you to recover, recover, and recover again. Remember, successful failure is not a bad thing. But if your failure is a sin, you must admit your failure to God, choose not to make the bad choice again, and return to walking with God. If you do these things, He promises to restore you.

6. When, in your life, have you experienced a successful failure? How did you learn from, and recover from, that failure?

_____

_____

7. Describe one or two or your unsuccessful failures? How did you learn from, and recover from the failure?

_____

_____

8. As a result of what you've learned in this session, how will you handle successful and unsuccessful failures differently in the future?

_____

_____

Do you think that Teknon will learn how to recover and get back into the battle? Press on to episode 9 of the story.

The Main Things I learned in this Champion Session are:

_____

_____

_____

_____

_____

CHAMPION
Sheet of Deeds

Go to the CHAMPION Sheet of Deeds on page 9 and write down **one thing you will begin to do** before the next session (and beyond) to apply the main things you learned in session 8.

Your Mission

Complete your mission and CHAMPION Session Prep before you meet for session 9.

Power Verse: Joshua 1:9

Date memorized: _____

Critical Maneuver

This will reinforce what you learned today. Obtain your maneuver instructions from your father.

CHAMPION Sheet of Deeds

Begin to apply your action point from your Sheet of Deeds.

CHAMPION Session Prep

Reread episode 9 of *Teknon and the CHAMPION Warriors*, and then complete session 9 in your *Mission Guide* on your own. **Our next CHAMPION Session:**

DATE:

_____

TIME:

_____

PLACE:

_____

♦ Teknon and the Champion Warriors ♦

Session 9:
Recover, Recover, Recover

CHAMPION Characteristics
Courage and Mental Toughness

POWER VERSE: PSALM 56:3-4

When I am afraid, I will put my trust in You. In God, whose word I praise, in God I have put my trust; I shall not be afraid. What can mere man do to me?

Discussion Topics

Breaking out of your "comfort zone"
Being respected vs. being liked
Recovering from failure—part 2: not giving in to discouragement

Mission Debrief

1. Discuss your mission from session 8. Did you complete your maneuver? If so, what did you learn? If not, why not?

_____

_____

2. What are some habits you are successfully forming as you apply your action points from your Sheet of Deeds? Any areas of struggle?

_____

_____

3. Recite your power verse (Joshua 1:9) from session 8.

4. What is your greatest fear from among those you identified during your mission from session 8? What are some things you could do to overcome it (remember, the CHAMPION's Ring includes areas where you can make a difference)? What things do you need to trust to the Lord (responsibilities that rest in God's Ring)?

_____

_____

_____

_____

5. Recite the CHAMPION Warrior Creed out loud. Pause before you say the lines about courage and mental toughness.

RECONNAISSANCE

1. Review the Map of the Mission on page 8 to determine the team's location in episode 9.

2. Review the CHAMPION definitions of **Courage** and **Mental Toughness** (refer to the CHAMPION Code on page 6).

_____

_____

_____

_____

OPTIONAL QUESTIONS

3. What were Matty's three main instructions to Teknon?

_____

_____

4. How did Teknon motivate the Phaskos to join him?

_____

_____

_____

5. Why did Teknon hesitate to go to the village? What was he afraid of?

_____

_____

6. Why did Tor tell Teknon not to worry about being liked by the Phaskos? What did Tor say about respect? What did he mean?

_____

_____

7. Look back at episode 4 where Teknon meets the Harpax. Do you think Teknon liked being liked? Why do you think acceptance by the Harpax was so important to Teknon?

_____

_____

8. What did Scandalon do to Teknon on his way to the village? Why?

_____

_____

9. What did Teknon recognize about the strange voice he heard while he was leading the Phaskos back to the team?

_____

_____

In the world you have tribulation, but take courage; I [Jesus] have overcome the world.

John 16:33b

10. Why did Teknon respond differently to Scandalon's voice on the way back to the clearing?

_____

_____

11. Why did Teknon want to keep the scar on his arm?

_____

_____

12. Do you think Teknon recovered from his failure in episode 8? If so, how?

_____

_____

STRATEGY AND TACTICS

Be on the alert, stand firm in the faith, act like men, be strong.

1 Corinthians 16:13

BREAK OUT OF THE ZONE!

Have you ever heard an athlete say, "I was in the zone"? For an athlete, being "in the zone" refers to playing a sport far beyond what he considers his normal ability. If you've had that experience, you know how good it feels to experience that kind of achievement. There's another zone, however, that also feels good, but for another reason. It's called the "comfort zone."

In the comfort zone, you feel good because you feel comfortable. The comfort zone is a place where you do things because it's the way you've always done them.

Let's say you are becoming a skilled trumpet player. One

morning the bandleader says to you, "How about playing a solo during our next concert?"

"No way," you blurt out. "I like playing with the other trumpet players just fine, thank you very much." There you are in the center of your comfort zone. You have an opportunity to grow, but you don't want to risk breaking out.

1. Have you ever been afraid to take on a particularly difficult task, to work closely with someone who really seems not to like you, or to ask for the help of someone who you are afraid to approach? Jot down a couple of examples.

_____

_____

We break out of our comfort zone by conquering our fears. When we conquer fears with God's help, we experience personal, emotional, and spiritual victory.

We will examine some important factors to remember when you want to break out of your comfort zone.

GOD PROVIDES THE POWER TO BREAK OUT OF THE ZONE

2a. What does King David tell you about who God is and what He does for you in Psalm 27:1,13-14?

_____

_____

_____

2b. What does Psalm 27:1,13-14 tell you not to do? What does it tell you that you should do?

_____

_____

Every noble work is at first impossible.

Thomas Carlyle

BREAKING OUT OF THE ZONE IS PROFITABLE BUT NOT ALWAYS POPULAR

Often, the biggest barrier to leaving the comfort zone is our own fear of what others might say. Nobody likes to be criticized, and nobody likes to be misunderstood. When we do something outside our comfort zone, like giving a speech or sharing our faith in God with someone else, we put our egos at risk. Let's face it: we like to be liked. But it is not always necessary to be liked by everyone. At times, people are going to misunderstand us. At other times, people will also become angry with us even when we do the right thing!

3. Read Psalm 56:3-4. If you trust in God, what can others do to you?

_____

_____

_____

_____

_____

4. What does Jesus warn us about living in this world in John 15:15-16? How should we expect to be liked and accepted if we are His friends and follow Him?

_____

_____

_____

_____

On May 20-21, 1927, Charles Lindbergh accomplished something many people thought was impossible. In fact, many people didn't understand why the young pilot would even attempt to fly solo across the Atlantic Ocean from New York to Paris. Today hundreds of planes fly transatlantic every day, but prior to 1927 several other pilots had met their deaths in similar transatlantic attempts. People tried to convince Lindbergh that death was waiting for him somewhere in the icy waters of the Atlantic. Many became angry and called him crazy. Fortunately, Lindbergh ignored his critics and showed the world that he and his famous plane, "The Spirit of St. Louis," had the right stuff. Today we recognize him as an American hero because of his unwillingness to allow circumstances or criticism to discourage him from reaching his dream.

In the same way, Scandalon hit Teknon with discouraging comments on his way to the village when he was trying to recover from failure. Our enemy (Satan) can use this tactic very effectively to keep us from recovering,

5. Do you ever hear voices like this from other people or in your own thoughts? Underline the following comments that sound familiar.

   ■ Don't tell me you're going to speak in front of the class today. Are you nuts?!
   ■ Forget trying out for the team. You don't stand a chance.
   ■ Why do you want to make good grades? No one else does.
   ■ You mean you haven't kissed a girl yet? What are you, some kind of freak?
   ■ Share your faith? What if the person laughs at you?

   Any others? Write them here:

   _____

As Teknon returned to the clearing, he recognized that Scandalon's voice was a trick. He determined that the voices he heard were a lie and did not apply to him. Then he changed his mental course by ignoring those false messages.

6. What does 2 Timothy 1:7 say about fear?

_____

_____

_____

_____

7. What does Jesus say about the truth (God's Word) in John 8:32?

_____

_____

_____

*We all are faced
with a series of
great opportun-
ities brilliantly
disguised as
impossible
situations.*

Charles Swindoll

When you hear false voices, replace them with the truth of God's Word. If you have invited Christ into your life by faith, you are a child of the King. Neither people nor Satan's messengers can intimidate you unless you let them.

According to Henry Blackaby and Claude King, authors of *Experiencing God*, God is working all around us. When we seek to develop our personal relationship with Him, which began when we invited Him into our lives by faith, He provides opportunities to join Him where He is working. These invitations usually take us out of our comfort zone. But if we step outside the zone (remember the CHAMPION's Ring on the Hoplon) and allow God to accomplish what only He can (God's Ring), we grow as individuals as well as in our relationship with Him.

Breaking Out of the Zone Is Worth the Risk

At times, God asks us to step out of our comfort zone to obey His will. We may not know how we are going to accomplish it, but we know that He wants it done. That's when God expects us to trust in Him by faith and watch Him bring about the results.

8. Read Matthew 17:20. If we have faith in God, what does He say that we can do? How much faith do we need in order to see God do mighty things?

_____

_____

_____

Everybody ought to do at least two things each day that he hates to do, just for practice.

Will James

We can have faith in God because He is faithful. He is all-powerful and loves you unconditionally. If God provides you an opportunity to leave your comfort zone, He will give you the power to break out of it. Philippians 4:13 reminds us that "I can do all things through Him [Jesus Christ] who gives me strength."

We grow by taking the risk to trust God in our daily lives. God loves us and wants us to grow—in our relationship with Him, in our understanding of ourselves, and in our relationships with other people. Just like Teknon received help to accomplish his rescue mission, we can trust God to provide the power to accomplish whatever mission He gives us when we ask for His help. We may not always see His answer right away. Sometimes God wants us to wait patiently; He wants us to learn through waiting, even though it's difficult. But we can always be confident that He knows our concerns and wants the best for us.

Remember when Tor told Teknon to look at his scar often, and never to forget what he had learned that night? Faith often involves risk—risk to our self-esteem and maybe even to our friendships. Sometimes we have to risk getting hurt by other people. But when we conquer our fears, step out of our comfort zone, and trust God through the experience, we will receive a feeling of exhilaration and a memory of victory that will stay with us forever!

9. Name three activities that would take you out of your comfort zone.

(1)

_____

(2)

_____

(3)

_____

◆ Teknon and the CHAMPION Warriors ◆

The Main Things I learned in this Champion Session are:

_____

_____

_____

_____

_____

You gain strength, courage, and confidence by every experience in which you really stop to look fear in the face ... You must do the thing you think you cannot do.

Eleanor Roosevelt

Champion
Sheet of Deeds

Go to the CHAMPION Sheet of Deeds on page 9 and write down **one thing you will begin to do** before the next session (and beyond) to apply the main things you learned in session 9.

Your Mission

Complete your mission and CHAMPION Session Prep before you meet for session 10.

Power Verse: Psalm 56:3-4

Date memorized: _____

Critical Maneuver

This will reinforce what you learned today. Obtain your maneuver instructions from your father.

CHAMPION Sheet of Deeds

Begin to apply your action point from your Sheet of Deeds.

─── CHAMPION Session Prep ───

Reread episode 10 of *Teknon and the CHAMPION Warriors*, and then complete the questions in session 10 in your *Mission Guide* on your own. Our next CHAMPION Session will be:

DATE:
_____

TIME:
_____

PLACE:
_____

Courage • Honor • Attitude • Mental toughness • Purity • Integrity • Ownership • Navigation

Session 10:
Good Enough

CHAMPION Characteristics
Attitude and Integrity

POWER VERSE: 1 Corinthians 9:24–25A

Do you not know that those who run in a race all run, but only one receives the prize? Run in such a way that you may win. Everyone who competes in the games exercises self-control in all things.

Discussion Topics

Pursuing excellence and resisting mediocrity
Managing your anger

Mission Debrief

1. Discuss your mission from session 9. What was the most important thing you learned from your maneuver?

   _____

   _____

2. Name one key thing that you have learned so far by applying your action points from the Sheet of Deeds.

   _____

   _____

3. Recite your power verse (Psalm 56:3-4) from session 9.

4. This power verse reveals that we should not fear people. Is there any person or group of people you fear? Why? What can you do to face this fear?

   _____

   _____

   _____

   _____

5. Recite the CHAMPION Warrior Creed together from memory (see page 5).

RECONNAISSANCE

1. Review the Map of the Mission on page 8 to determine the team's location in episode 10.

2. Review the CHAMPION definition of **Integrity**.

_____

_____

_____

_____

3. What does the phrase "I will allow other people to hold me accountable to standards of excellence" mean to you?

_____

_____

_____

4. Phil said that the Northrons enjoyed mediocrity. How is this revealed in their lives?

_____

_____

_____

5. Tor said that the Northrons "have no vision ... no purpose ... no plan." He said, "Where there's no purpose, there's no passion for living." Why is it important to have vision, purpose, and a plan in our lives?

_____

_____

_____

Hold yourself responsible to a higher standard than anyone else expects of you. Never excuse yourself.

Henry Ward Beecher

Optional Questions

6. *Northros*, a Greek term, refers to being slothful, sluggish, or lazy. Why was this community called Northros?

_____

7. Why did Tor lose his temper?

_____

_____

8. Do you think that Tor had a right to get angry? Why or why not? Was it right for him to hurt the Northron? Why do you see it that way?

_____

_____

9. How did Tor feel after he lost his temper? What did he do after he hurt the Northron? Why?

_____

_____

_____

10. What did Epps say was a sign of true strength in Tor? What did Epps mean by that?

_____

_____

11. *Tharreo* is a Greek word that refers to having courage, confidence, and boldness. Tor is a task-driven leader; one who likes to be in authority. How does he show his courage?

_____

_____

The best preparation for tomorrow is doing your best today.

H. Jackson Brown, Jr.

Strategy and Tactics

Raise the Bar, Rock the Boat, but Don't Roll With the Tide

You decide to make better grades this semester. To make this happen, you will need to work harder and pay more attention in class. When your friends find out what you're doing, what might they say?

"JUST CHILL OUT!"

You choose to get into excellent physical shape. You will have to run and work out with weights three times a week. Some of your friends who don't exercise hear about this. What might they say?

"JUST CHILL OUT!"

You sense that God wants you to share your faith with some non-Christians. But in order to do that, you'll need to learn how to share your testimony of how you became a Christian, as well as how to lead another person into a relationship with Jesus.

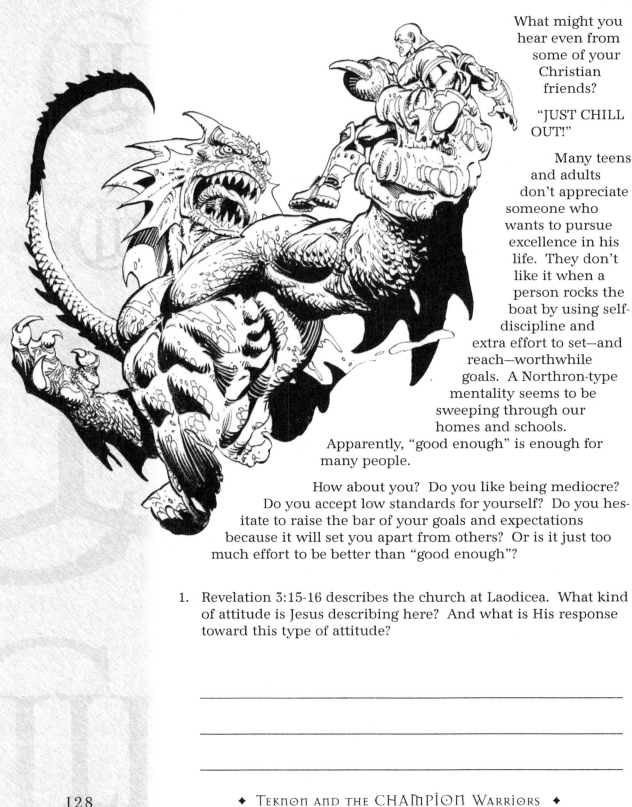

What might you hear even from some of your Christian friends?

"JUST CHILL OUT!"

Many teens and adults don't appreciate someone who wants to pursue excellence in his life. They don't like it when a person rocks the boat by using self-discipline and extra effort to set—and reach—worthwhile goals. A Northron-type mentality seems to be sweeping through our homes and schools. Apparently, "good enough" is enough for many people.

How about you? Do you like being mediocre? Do you accept low standards for yourself? Do you hesitate to raise the bar of your goals and expectations because it will set you apart from others? Or is it just too much effort to be better than "good enough"?

1. Revelation 3:15-16 describes the church at Laodicea. What kind of attitude is Jesus describing here? And what is His response toward this type of attitude?

    _____

    _____

    _____

2a. According to Ephesians 5:15-17, how should we use our time?

_____

_____

_____

2b. What do you think it means to "make the most of every opportunity"?

_____

_____

_____

Let us run with endurance the race that is set before us.

Hebrews 12:1b

3. Read Luke 2:40-52. In what ways was Jesus growing as a person even though He was only 12 years old?

_____

_____

_____

God expects us to be thankful for the talents and opportunities He gives us. He also expects us to make the most of the life and gifts He has provided. The story in Luke 2 declares that Jesus grew and kept increasing in stature (physically), in wisdom (mentally), in favor with men (socially), and in favor with God (spiritually). Jesus was a good steward of what God the Father had entrusted to Him. He set an example for us to keep increasing in our maturity by avoiding mediocrity in our lives.

4. In Matthew 19:26 what does Jesus say is possible with God?

_____

_____

5. Read Philippians 4:13. If we are Christians, what can we do as a result of God's power working through us?

_____

_____

Average is your enemy.

Pearce "Rocky" Lane

If nothing is impossible with God, and you can do all things through Him as He gives you His strength, how should you approach your activities? Ask yourself these questions:

■ Am I trying to learn everything that I can at school?

■ Do I do my chores at home completely, without grumbling?

■ Am I exercising and being careful about what I eat?

■ Am I reading good books on a regular basis?

■ Am I learning how to interact well with people and treating them kindly?

■ Am I consistent in spending time with God in prayer and Bible reading?

■ Do I know how to share my faith?

■ Do I look for opportunities to share my faith?

These questions refer to attitudes and behaviors that are your responsibility within the CHAMPION's Ring (see session 1). You can and should take responsibility to make the right choices in areas such as study, work, exercise, learning, and so on.

Don't allow yourself to fall into the Northron "good enough" mentality and don't be afraid to rock the boat of mediocrity. God will do His part (God's Ring), so trust Him to help you raise the bar in the different areas of your life. You don't have to roll with the tide of what everybody else is doing. "Aim high," as the Air Force says. Pursue excellence and let someone else do the chilling out!

USE YOUR HEAD; DON'T LOSE YOUR HEAD!

Do you have a short fuse? When people disagree with you or fail to meet your expectations does your response resemble the fireworks display at Walt Disney World? How often do you lose your patience or "blow up" with other people?

It's almost fashionable to have a short fuse, isn't it? More and more people seem to be adopting the attitude of "I'm mad and I'm not going to take it anymore!" as their creed for social interaction. Even violent anger is recognized as the status quo.

OPTIONAL QUESTIONS

6a. What makes you angry? How do you handle it when it erupts?

_____

6b. Does any particular person make you angry? Why? How do you handle it when this person makes you angry?

_____

_____

7. Review the CHAMPION definition of Attitude (refer to "The CHAMPION Code" on page 6).

_____

_____

---

8. How do you think a person learns to manage anger?

_____

_____

The Bible talks about the process of managing anger as a key component of self-control. Self-control is one of the outward expressions of Christ's presence in our lives as we learn to entrust our lives to Him. The Bible calls these characteristics the "fruit of the Spirit."

9. Read Galatians 5:22-23. What is the fruit of the Spirit?

_____

_____

_____

_____

Speak when you're angry, and you'll make the best speech you'll ever regret.

Anonymous

Uncontrolled anger, like so many other things, can become a habit. Once you get used to "losing your head" it becomes easier to let it happen the next time. Tor had a habit of losing his temper until he decided to become a CHAMPION Warrior. He knew that self-control was a key characteristic of a CHAMPION and didn't want to accept "good enough" in his life.

If you are a Christian, God expects you to overcome a bad temper by drawing on His power. We plug into His strength by being filled with His Spirit. When you are filled with the Holy Spirit, you start displaying the fruit of the Spirit. It is one thing to hate evil and become angered by its presence in the world. It's another thing to take out frustrations on others. When we do that, we disobey God. If you sense that you have disobeyed God through a fit of bad temper, remember 1 John 1:9 and confess your anger to Him. He will forgive you and reestablish His line of communication and power with you.

But we could spend our lives trying to manage anger after it has erupted. How do we keep from losing our temper ahead of time? The book of James describes an effective formula for anger prevention.

10. Read James 1:19-20. What three things should we do to keep from losing our temper?

Write the formula here:

God's Power + _____ + _____

+ _____ = Anger Management

Emmett John Hughes, a friend of former President Eisenhower gave him this advice: "Never miss an opportunity to keep your mouth shut."

Keeping our mouths shut is one of the hardest things in the world to do when we get upset. It's also one of the most effective tools in anger management. A spoken word is like a football right before it's intercepted. As much as the quarterback wants it back, he can't get it back. If there is any question whether or not you should say something, listen to what Mr. Hughes said to the president. DON'T SAY IT!

Instead of being quick to speak, use the other highly effective tool in anger management. Learn to listen. Author Stephen Covey says, "Seek first to understand, then to be understood." Listen not only to what's being said, but also to what isn't being said. Try to put yourself in the other person's shoes so you can better understand his or her position.

God knows that you get angry; He created anger to alert you that something is wrong. But when you get angry, draw on His strength to remain calm and under the control of His Spirit. Use your head; don't lose your head!

The Main Things I learned in this Champion Session are:

_____

_____

_____

_____

_____

Don't fly into a rage unless you are prepared for a rough landing.

Anonymous

CHAMPION
SHEET OF DEEDS

Go to the CHAMPION Sheet of Deeds on page 9 and write down **one thing you will begin to do** before the next session (and beyond) to apply the main things you learned in session 10.

Your Mission

Complete your mission and CHAMPION Session Prep before you meet for session 11.

Power verse: I Corinthians 9:24-25a

Date memorized: _____

Critical Maneuver

Your father will give you instructions for your maneuver.

CHAMPION Sheet of Deeds

Begin to apply your action point from your Sheet of Deeds.

CHAMPION Session Prep

Reread episode 11 of *Teknon and the CHAMPION Warriors*, and then complete the questions in session 11 of your *Mission Guide* on your own. **Our next CHAMPION Session will be:**

DATE:

_____

TIME:

_____

PLACE:

_____

◆ Teknon and the CHAMPION Warriors ◆

COURAGE • HONOR • ATTITUDE • MENTAL TOUGHNESS • PURITY • INTEGRITY • OWNERSHIP • NAVIGATION

SESSION 11:
THE ELEMENT OF DOUBT

CHAMPION Characteristics
Integrity and Purity

POWER VERSE: 1 THESSALONIANS 5:21-22

But examine everything carefully; hold fast to that which is good; abstain from every form of evil.

Discussion Topics

Knowing who I am and what my personal convictions are
Living out my convictions
Avoiding romantic relationships and entanglements

Mission debrief

1. Discuss your mission from session 10. What was the most important thing you learned from your maneuver?

   _____

   _____

2. What changes are happening in your life as you apply your action points from the CHAMPION Sheet of Deeds? Share some victories you are seeing.

   _____

   _____

3. Recite your power verse (1 Corinthians 9:24-25a) from session 10.

4. Name at least one area in which you have executed self-control since your last CHAMPION session.

   _____

   _____

5. Recite the CHAMPION Warrior Creed from memory. If you can, invite two or more people to be in the room when you say it.

RECONNAISSANCE

1. Review the Map of the Mission on page 8 before beginning this section. Identify where the team is located in episode 11.

2. Review the CHAMPION definitions of **Integrity** and **Purity** (refer to the CHAMPION Code on page 6).

_____

_____

_____

_____

_____

3. How did Magos try to confuse Teknon?

_____

_____

_____

4. What did Magos offer Teknon?

_____

_____

_____

_____

5. Why do you think Magos challenged Teknon about his beliefs? What did Epps have to say about this?

_____

_____

_____

_____

_____

Magos wanted to create doubt in your mind about your beliefs, so that you would feel frightened and insecure.

Epps

6. Why did Teknon enjoy spending time with Pary?

_____

_____

7. In what way(s) did Teknon's encounter with Magos affect his decision to see Pary again?

_____

_____

8. Describe how Teknon treated Pary during the three days they spent together.

_____

_____

9. After his conversation with Epps, what did Teknon realize that he had done wrong?

_____

_____

_____

◆ Teknon and the CHAMPION Warriors ◆

10. How did Pary respond when Teknon talked with her that last morning on the beach? Why did she react this way?

_____

_____

_____

11. How could Teknon have prevented this from happening and still maintained his friendship with Pary?

_____

_____

STRATEGY AND TACTICS

Failure to prepare is preparing to fail.

John Wooden

BE WILLING TO GET A BLOODY NOSE

Several years ago, a guy in his twenties named Brad got a job with a medical company selling surgical equipment. He spent the first six weeks training with that company in Chicago, learning everything he could about how to sell his company's products to hospitals and surgeons. One day during training, the vice-president sat down with Brad in the cafeteria. Trying to make conversation, Brad asked, "What would you do if you were starting out as a salesman again?" The executive's response was simple:

"I'd get out in the field and get my nose bloody. That's the way you learn this business."

What was he saying to Brad? Did the vice-president mean that his new salesman should go back and try to start fights with doctors? No, he didn't have enough insurance for that! The executive was telling the young salesman that he needed to talk with his customers, try to meet the customers' needs, face stiff competition from other salesmen, allow himself to get challenged about what he had learned in training, and be willing to fail a few times as he started his new career. The vice-president knew that challenge isn't a bad thing. Challenge is a good thing.

An expert at anything was once a beginner.

H. Jackson Browne

1. Have you ever felt overly confident about a particular subject or task?

    _____

    _____

Author and speaker Stephen Covey often says, "Confidence is what you have before you understand the problem." It's important for each of us to realize that when we start out doing something new and important, we'll probably be challenged. Even if we feel confident about what we are learning, we don't know how *little* we know until we get *challenged* about what we know. When we get challenged on a topic, like Magos challenged Teknon, we have a great opportunity to reaffirm what we believe about that topic and to identify the things we don't know about it. Once we learn what we don't know, we can go and find the answers we need.

Magos gave Teknon a "bloody nose" by confusing him about his beliefs and convictions. Teknon became flustered and upset because he allowed Magos to inject the element of doubt into his mind. And because Teknon didn't immediately have an answer for Magos, he lost his confidence. Could Teknon have prevented Magos from frightening him like that?

A temptation to compromise your standards often comes when your beliefs are challenged. Let's look at another person who was challenged and offered a proposition by someone evil like Magos.

2a. Read Luke 4:1-13. Who was challenged? —and by whom?

_____

_____

2b. Considering that Jesus ate nothing during His time in the desert (verses 1-2), how do you think He felt when He was being challenged?

_____

_____

2c. How did Jesus respond to the temptations and challenges made to Him?

Verses to consider	Temptation/Challenge	Jesus' response
Luke 4:3-4		
Luke 4:5-8		
Luke 4:9-12		

Reject passivity, accept responsibility, lead courageously, and expect God's reward.

Robert Lewis

Jesus was very tired and hungry when Satan challenged His beliefs. But instead of becoming unsettled when Satan tried to use the element of doubt, Jesus quoted Scripture to strengthen his position. He confidently relied on the words of His Heavenly Father.

If you have accepted Jesus as your personal Savior by faith, sooner or later you will get challenged about why you believe in Jesus. If that happens, great! You will have the opportunity to go back to the Bible to find the answers to the challenges given to you. By doing that, you will fuel your confidence and reinforce your position in Christ! If you need help, ask your parents, your pastor, or someone else whom you respect to point you to Bible verses and other Bible-based materials that apply to your situation.

Better yet, even when someone else is *not* challenging you, spend time reading and studying the Bible now so that you will become more knowledgeable about what it means to be a Christian and apply God's truth each day.

3. Most everyone has asked himself or herself, "What will my friends think if I stand up for what I believe?" Why is that such an important question to us?

_____

_____

_____

Build your character based on what God's Word has to say about His character. Don't get rattled like Teknon. He got stressed out over Magos' challenge, decided to take a break from reality in order to make himself feel better, and hurt himself and Pary in the process ... which leads us to our second topic.

AVOID THE GUSH!

Here's what God says about relationships:

"Learn to love appropriately. You need to use your head and test your feelings so that your love is sincere and intelligent, not sentimental gush." Philippians 1:9-10 (The Message)

4. It's nice when a girl shows you affection, isn't it? What could be more pleasant than when she calls you on the phone and tells you how great you are? It makes you feel good, doesn't it? But when you feel that way, whose needs are you meeting—yours or hers? Are you being sincere and intelligent, or are you giving in to sentimental gush?

_____

_____

_____

Emotions can be weird and funny things. When emotions get involved in a relationship between a young man and a young woman, friends start to become more than friends. Often at that point people start getting hurt.

5a. Read 1 Timothy 5:1-2. How are you supposed to treat young women if you will honor her and honor God?

_____

_____

_____

_____

5b. Is it wise for me to be anything other than a friend to what the Bible calls my sisters in the Lord? Why or why not?

_____

_____

_____

_____

_____

In his excellent book, *I Kissed Dating Goodbye*, Joshua Harris has this to say about romantic relationships:

> "I've come to realize that I have no business asking for a girl's heart and affections if I'm not ready to back up my request with a lifelong commitment. Until I can do that, I'd only be using that woman to meet my short-term needs, not seeking to bless her for the long term."

A **lifelong commitment**??? *Wait a minute!* you may be thinking. *I'm not talking about a lifelong commitment! I just want to talk on the phone for a while. Or go to the movies. Or out to eat. Just have a little fun.*

Sounds crazy doesn't it? But even now, if you're not careful, you can misuse a romantic relationship with a young woman in order to meet your short-term needs instead of blessing her for the long term. Remember Teknon and Pary? Teknon just wanted to get away from it all for a few days. But instead, a "perceived" romantic relationship was created and Pary was hurt as a result.

The pressure to start dating and to begin relationships is occurring earlier in life than ever before. Don't allow yourself to start something romantic that you can't and shouldn't finish. Instead, seek to treat young women as cherished sisters, friends whom you can encourage. Don't get caught up in the gush because there is so much more to enjoy at this point by being friends. This delayed gratification (waiting for what I want until God gives it to me at the right time) will become tougher as the years go by, but God will bless you for making the right decisions. And your effort will be greatly rewarded—beyond whatever you could ask or think! God promises this in Ephesians 3:20. Check it out.

6. What do you think would cause a girl to like you?

    _____

7. Describe what you think a friendship with a girl should be like.

    _____

    _____

    _____

The Main Things I learned in this Champion Session are:

_____

_____

_____

_____

_____

The gem cannot be polished without friction, nor man perfected with scars.

Chinese Proverb

CHAMPION
Sheet of Deeds

Go to The CHAMPION Sheet of Deeds on page 9 and write down **one thing you will begin to do** before the next session (and beyond) to apply the main things you learned in session 11.

Your Mission

Complete your mission and CHAMPION Session Prep before you meet for session 12.

POWER VERSE: 1 THESSALONIANS 5:21-22

Date memorized: _____

CRITICAL MANEUVER

This will reinforce what you learned in this session. Obtain your maneuver instructions from your father.

CHAMPION SHEET OF DEEDS

Begin to apply your action point from your Sheet of Deeds.

CHAMPION SESSION PREP

Reread Episode 12 of *Teknon and the CHAMPION Warriors*, and then complete the questions in Session 12 in your *Mission Guide* on your own. **Our next CHAMPION Session will be:**

DATE:
_____

TIME:
_____

PLACE:
_____

CourAGE · HonoR · AttitUDE · MENTAL TOUGHNESS · PURity · INtEGRITY · OWNERSHIP · NAVIGATION

SESSiON 12:
NOTHiNG MoRE,
NOTHiNG LEss,
NOTHiNG ELsE

CHAMPiON CHARACTERISTIC
Attitude

POWER VERSE: 1 CORiNTHiAns 15:57–58

But thanks be to God, who gives us the victory through our Lord Jesus Christ. Therefore, my beloved brethren, be steadfast, immovable, always abounding in the work of the Lord, knowing that your toil is not in vain in the Lord.

Managing discouragement

Keeping circumstances and self-perception
in proper perspective

Drawing on God's strength and wisdom

Mission Debrief

1. Discuss your mission from session 11. What did you learn from your maneuver? Has your attitude or behavior changed as a result of your maneuver?

_____

_____

2. Are you experiencing any struggles as you apply your action points from the CHAMPION Sheet of Deeds? If so, please share these.

_____

_____

3. Recite your power verse (1 Thessalonians 5:21-22) from session 11.

4. Our last session explored the topic of romantic relationships. Do you have a romantic relationship with a young woman right now? If so, should the relationship continue as it is? Why or why not?

_____

_____

_____

5. Recite all of the CHAMPION Warrior Creed from memory (see page 5).

RECONNAISSANCE

1. Review the Map of the Mission on page 8 and determine the team's location in episode 12.

2. Review the CHAMPION definition of **Attitude** (refer to the CHAMPION Code on page 6).

_____

_____

_____

3. What were some of the reasons Teknon became frustrated and angry?

_____

_____

4. What were some of the things that contributed to Teknon's discouragement?

_____

_____

_____

_____

_____

_____

5. How did Teknon act when he became discouraged? Be specific.

   _____

6. What, according to Kratos and Phil, is the way to overcome discouragement?

   _____

   _____

   _____

7. Phil told Teknon, "Even when our emotions tell us otherwise, we must stay focused on trusting Pneuma to help us make the right choices." Do you think our emotions are dependable? Why or why not?

   _____

   _____

Strategy and Tactics

Former fighter pilot, Charlie Plumb says that it was the parachute packers in his life who pulled him through the loneliness and discouragement he faced during his six years as a prisoner of war during the Vietnam conflict. Charlie, now a popular seminar speaker, states that he is continually thankful for the man who carefully assembled his parachute aboard the USS *Kittyhawk* on the day his airplane was shot down over enemy territory.

But Charlie is quick to add that he is even more thankful for his cellmates in the concentration camp who carefully helped him pack his emotional, mental, and spiritual parachutes. Due to the constant help and encouragement that these extraordinary men provided, Charlie not only survived his imprisonment but also returned home a stronger person.

Soon, you will have the dubious pleasure of "flying" into an uncharted territory known as young adulthood. While you pilot through peer pressure, relating to young women, school challenges, and the other struggles of daily life, you may be "shot down" by discouragement. Your emotional health may be affected by a number of things, including your family, friends, diet, sleep patterns, and, of course, your relationship with God.

Discouragement can become a big gaping hole in your spiritual parachute. At some point, you will probably need a spiritual "parachute packer" who can encourage you as you face the enemy fire of confusion, isolation, and discouragement during your teens and into young adulthood. Use this opportunity to build a stronger relationship with your father. You can also ask your dad or pastor to identify men who could encourage you during your teenage years. Remember, they've been there, so they know what it's like to be shot down, to regroup, and then to take off again.

1a. List those people who are emotional and spiritual "parachute packers" in your life.

_____

_____

1b. How do these people support you?

_____

_____

THE POWER OF HOPE

A few years ago, scientists conducted an experiment on hope. They took a common rat and put it into a large bowl of water. Then they watched as the rat swam around the edge of the bowl for days, staying afloat and trying to find a way to get out.

Then the scientists started the second phase of the study. They removed the first rat and put another rat into the same bowl of water, but this time they turned off all the lights in the room. Left to swim in total darkness, the second rat drowned in only a few hours, greatly surprising the scientists. Why did this rat die so quickly? The scientists concluded that it simply gave up hope. Without visual contact, the second rat had no vision of the outside world—and thus had lost all hope of survival.

Can you identify with the second rat? Have you ever felt as if you were swimming for your life in a dark bowl full of peer pressure, challenging relationships, and stressful activities? As if you could barely keep your head above water? If so, you're not alone. Many people face the darkness of discouragement.

Victory belongs to the most persevering.

Napoleon

2. List some of the possible characteristics of a discouraged person.

    1. _____

    2. _____

    3. _____

    4. _____

    5. _____

3. List some things that you think would cause someone to feel discouraged.

    1. _____

    2. _____

    3. _____

    4. _____

    5. _____

◆ Teknon and the CHAMPION Warriors ◆

Many things can cause us to feel discouraged and cause us to start going downhill emotionally. The more we get discouraged and lose hope, the farther down we go. Let's look at several categories of downhills that can cause discouragement.

CATEGORY 1: HEALTH DOWNHILLS

▲ **Lack of sleep**. Former President Teddy Roosevelt said, "Fatigue makes cowards of us all." If we don't get enough sleep, we can become irritable and start to "cycle down."

▲ **Bad diet**. Too much sugar, caffeine, and fat can wreak havoc on our minds and our emotional stability.

▲ **Lack of exercise**. When we exercise, blood pumps oxygen into our blood and sends hormones called endorphins through our bodies to make us feel alert and energetic. When we spend too much time being a couch potato, we feel and act like sedated slugs.

CATEGORY 2: HEAD DOWNHILLS

▲ **Criticism from peers**. Overly critical people can have a negative effect on our attitudes and actions.

▲ **"Successful" failure**. We can become discouraged when we fail at doing the right things, like trying our best but still losing the game.

▲ **Stress**. Too much activity makes us feel like we're under the pile and unable to dig out.

CATEGORY 3: HEART DOWNHILLS

▲ **Unresolved conflict**. If we haven't reconnected with friends or family after an argument, we will experience a lack of closure until the problem is resolved.

▲ **"Unsuccessful" failure**. When we make a bad choice and disobey God (sin), we will feel miserable.

▲ **Unconfessed sin**. When we don't acknowledge to God that we have sinned and ask His forgiveness, guilt and discouragement will follow.

A real leader faces the music, even when he doesn't like the tune.

Unknown

Teknon's discouragement related to all three of these categories. He was tired and hungry. He had unresolved conflict with Pary. In addition, Magos had confused him with criticism of the CHAMPION principles, causing him to doubt his beliefs and to have a bad attitude toward Pneuma and their mission. All of these circumstances prompted him to lose hope and start riding the downhill of discouragement.

4. How might Teknon have avoided becoming discouraged?

_____

_____

5. What kind of things get you down emotionally or spiritually?

_____

_____

_____

6. Is there anything bothering you that you need to discuss with God? If so, what do you plan to do?

_____

_____

_____

There's a lot you can do to dodge discouragement. *To avoid the health downhills*, you need to eat right, get enough sleep, and get on a regular exercise program. *To avoid the head downhills*, you should try not to spend too much time with negative people. You should also recover when you have an "unsuccessful" failure and prioritize your time by involving yourself in only a few activities at a time.

As for avoiding the heart downhills, you should make sure that you are doing what you can to clear up unresolved arguments with others. Most importantly, you need to remember the importance of staying in communication with Jesus Christ. If you have unconfessed sin in your life, the phone lines are cut between you and God. You need to remember how to reconnect those communication lines through confession and turning away from your sin and toward God (repentance).

7a. Remember 1 John 1:9? What does that verse say we need to do if we have disobeyed God?

_____

_____

7b. What does God promise to do in return?

_____

_____

The longer we ride the downhill of discouragement, the more we take our eyes off the One who can help us. Soon, we start losing hope and forgetting about the big picture. God doesn't want us to become discouraged.

8. You looked at Hebrews 12:1-2 in an earlier session. Look at it again, but this time focus on the first part of verse 2: "fixing our eyes on Jesus, the author and perfecter of faith ... " These verses talk about how we run the race of life that God has marked out for us and how we run to win. What is the big key to success that you find in verse 2?

_____

_____

_____

_____

9a. According to John 10:10, what kind of life does He want us to live?

_____

_____

_____

> _Until you do what you believe in, you don't know whether you believe it or not._
>
> Leo Tolstoy

9b. What does the concept of abundant life or life lived to the full mean to you?

_____

_____

_____

_____

God wants each of us to live a meaningful, significant, maximum kind of life. He understands when you become discouraged, but He also knows that you don't have to stay that way. Take the right steps to get off of the downhill, and start riding the Abundant Life Express transport that God has for you!

The Main Things I learned in this Champion Session are:

_____

_____

_____

_____

_____

CHAMPION
Sheet of Deeds

Go to the CHAMPION Sheet of Deeds on page 9 and write down **one thing you will begin to do** before the next session (and beyond) to apply the main things you learned in session 12.

Your Mission

Complete your mission and CHAMPION Session Prep before you meet for session 13.

Power Verse: 1 Corinthians 15:57–58

Date memorized: _____

Critical Maneuver

This will reinforce what you learned in this session. Obtain your maneuver instructions from your father.

CHAMPION Sheet of Deeds

Begin to apply your action point from your Sheet of Deeds.

CHAMPION Session Prep

Reread episode 13 of *Teknon and the CHAMPION Warriors*, and then complete the questions in session 13 in your *Mission Guide* on your own. **Our next CHAMPION Session will be:**

DATE:

_____

TIME:

_____

PLACE:

_____

CoURAGE • HONOR • ATTITUDE • MENTAL TOUGHNESS • PURITY • INTEGRITY • OWNERSHIP • NAVIGATION

SESSION 13:
A JOB TO FINSIH

CHAMPION Characteristics

Mental Toughness and Navigation

POWER VERSE: PHILIPPIANS 3:13B-14

Forgetting what lies behind and reaching forward to what lies ahead, I press on toward the goal for the prize of the upward call of God in Christ Jesus.

Discussion Topics

Choosing to focus on the mission
Learning to persevere even in difficult circumstances
Connecting with God and drawing on His power

Mission Debrief

1. Discuss your mission from session 12. What did you learn from your maneuver? How is what you've learned affecting your attitude or behavior?

   _____

   _____

2. Did you start applying your new action point from your Sheet of Deeds? If so, what have you learned? If not, when do you plan to get started?

   _____

   _____

3. Recite your power verse (1 Corinthians 15:57-58) from session 12.

4. In our last session, we discussed the topic of discouragement. Have you dealt with any discouragement this week? If so, how did you handle it? If not, what helped you to avoid feeling discouraged?

   _____

   _____

   _____

5. Recite the CHAMPION Warrior Creed (see page 5).

Reconnaissance

1. Review the Map of the Mission on page 8 and determine the team's location in episode 13.

2. Review the CHAMPION definition of **Mental Toughness**.

_____

_____

_____

3. Why did Teknon decide to complete the mission on his own after he defeated the amacho?

_____

_____

4. Why do you think Teknon decided to talk with Pneuma?

_____

_____

_____

5. How did Teknon make the Hoplon fly?

_____

_____

Teknon really learned to focus in this episode, didn't he? He focused in order to get back on the track of completing his mission. Did you notice how much more confident Teknon became after using his training to defeat the amacho and Rhegma? Did you notice his resolve and inner strength after he finally connected with Pneuma on a personal level?

Strategy and Tactics

The Power of Focus

In the early 1900s, the United States needed a capable athlete to compete in the pentathlon, the most difficult track-and-field event of the fifth Olympiad. After much debate, the Olympic committee chose an unlikely candidate for an unlikely reason. The competitor they chose was a young army lieutenant who had displayed marginal competence in only one of the five events needed to win the pentathlon. What he lacked in ability, however, he made up with intensity. He was chosen to compete because of his determination and his focus.

He had one month to prepare for the event. During that short period of time, the focused army officer trained with unbridled passion. He forced his body to perform far beyond its normal limitations. He made it his mission to represent his country in an admirable fashion. Amazingly, he almost won a medal competing against the greatest athletes in the world. The name of the young lieutenant was George S. Patton, future four-star general of the American Armed Forces. He later became famous for his focus and determination as the leader of the Third Army that helped to defeat Hitler during World War II.

1. Are you able to focus so that you can complete a task even under stressful conditions? Would you say you are strong or need to improve a little, or need to improve a lot? Why do you say that?

    _____

    _____

A Mark of Maturity

Pastor and author Dr. Joel Hunter says that one of the most telling marks of maturity in a person is his ability to focus on the completion of a worthy task. The ability to focus is becoming a lost art for many young people today. For the most part, our fast-

Nobody who ever gave his best regretted it.

George Halas

paced, entertainment-obsessed society does not see the need nor are they equipped to develop this important character trait.

Three primary things can disrupt our focus as we attempt to accomplish worthwhile objectives:

1. **Complications.** These are the problems and obstacles that come our way.

2. **Criticism.** Negative and severe judgments can come from other people or from ourselves. Criticism is an occupational hazard for a person who sets high standards for himself.

3. **Circumstances.** Usually these focus-busters come in the form of opposition against a worthwhile objective.

In the movie "October Sky," high school student Homer Hickam gazed up with amazement into a clear West Virginia night. His eyes were fixed on *Sputnik I*, the world's first orbiting satellite that was shooting across the atmosphere at 17,000 miles per hour. At that moment, he made a decision that would affect the rest of his life. He decided to build rockets.

The idea seemed impossible to everyone who knew him. Homer grew up in a small coal-mining town in which most men spent long working days a hundred feet below the earth's surface. Homer and his friends were expected to follow the same career path into the mines as soon as they graduated from high school. But Homer had a different set of dreams to pursue.

Homer and his three companions decided to build a miniature rocket in the hope of winning the national science fair. They dedicated themselves to learning physics, math, and chemistry. Step by step, enduring failure after failure, Homer and his friends moved closer to their goal. In 1957, against incredible odds, the "Rocket Boys," as they were later called, came in first place in the national science fair and went on to achieve what they wanted most. They all continued to work hard and graduated from college.

What was so special about the Rocket Boys? Why did they succeed in achieving their dreams—overcoming all the obstacles that stopped others? It's because they took responsibility to do what they could do, and they focused on completing their objectives under very difficult conditions.

The Rocket Boys studied, worked hard, and never took their focus off of their objective. That's why Homer Hickam went on to train astronauts for NASA.

2. Look up the word "focus" in the dictionary. How would you define focus in your own words?

_____

_____

_____

When a person can maintain his concentration and direct his efforts long enough to complete an important task regardless of the obstacles, he is revealing a mature mark of manhood. He's acting like a CHAMPION by doing all he can within his own CHAMPION's Ring and trusting God for the results.

Remembering the Lion and the Bear

The Bible tells about a young man who also focused in order to complete his mission under difficult conditions. His name was David and his "super-sized" mission was defeating a giant named Goliath.

Read 1 Samuel 17:1-54

3a. Describe Goliath (verses 4-11 and 43-44).

_____

_____

_____

_____

3b. How did David view Goliath (verse 26 and 46)?

_____

_____

3c. Why did David believe that he could defeat Goliath
(verses 34-37 and 47)?

_____

_____

*Success seems to be
largely a matter of
hanging on after
others have let go.*

Will Feather

3d. Why did David refuse to wear King Saul's armor (verses 38-40)?

_____

_____

3e. According to 1 Samuel 17:45-47, how did David feel about completing his mission? Circle the number on the following scale that best describes his level of confidence.

0   1   2   3   4   5   6   7   8   9   10

Very Worried   Very Confident

3f. What did David use to defeat Goliath (verses 40 and 47-50)?

_____

_____

_____

David was willing to face Goliath because he—a shepherd boy—remembered how God had delivered him from the lion and the bear in the fields of Israel. David knew that God was watching over him and protecting him.

Do you realize that God is watching over you 24/7 (24 hours a day, 7 days a week) to protect you? Psalm 121:7 gives you a great promise: "The Lord will protect you from all evil; He will keep your soul."

How to Focus

Let's use David's example to discover some practical steps you can use to focus on completing important missions in your life.

- **Target your objective.** David targeted Goliath as the adversary he had to defeat for God and his country.
- **Train yourself for the mission.** David trained himself by conditioning both physically and spiritually during his time as a shepherd.
- **Think of the resources** you will need to complete the mission. David carefully chose his method and the tools he needed to ensure Goliath's defeat.
- **Trust that God will use and empower you** to complete any mission that He has given you. David acknowledged at an early age that his strength came from the Lord.
- **Thank God** for His faithful commitment to provide for you so that you can complete the mission. It is very important to remember how God has been faithful to you in the past. David expressed his gratitude to God for delivering him from the lion and the bear and then from Goliath.
- **Take action to complete your mission.** David acted upon his trust in God by stepping onto the battlefield. Once he made the first step to confront Goliath, there was no turning back. The Bible says that David actually charged toward Goliath on the battlefield.

It's easy to become distracted from doing the important things in our lives. Sometimes even good things can prevent us from doing the best things—those things that will make the greatest long-term impact. For example, too many basketball games or too much time with friends might prevent us from spending time reading the Bible or finishing our homework.

To become a CHAMPION, you must learn to prioritize your objectives wisely. Then you must focus your mind, your time, and your resources to complete the most important objectives before moving on to the other ones. It won't be easy. But when you look

The will to win is important, but the will to prepare is vital.

Joe Paterno

at guys like David, or Homer Hickam, you can see the benefits of learning how to focus.

4. What if you don't want to complete an important objective? How do you get it done if you just don't feel like it?

_____

_____

Sometimes you need to have the "want to" when it comes to completing a worthy objective. Sometimes, however, God directs you to achieve an important objective that is not fun or pleasant. If maturity can be identified by your ability to focus, then you show your level of maturity by your willingness to trust God, even through a task that offers little enjoyment through the process of completion.

5a. Which important objectives do you have that you find pretty easy to accomplish?

_____

_____

5b. Which ones are tough and demand all the focus you can muster in order to get them done?

_____

_____

5c. In what ways might God be able to help you face—and achieve—difficult objectives in your life?

_____

_____

_____

_____

The greatest honor we can give Almighty God is to live gladly because of the knowledge of His love.

Julian of Norwich

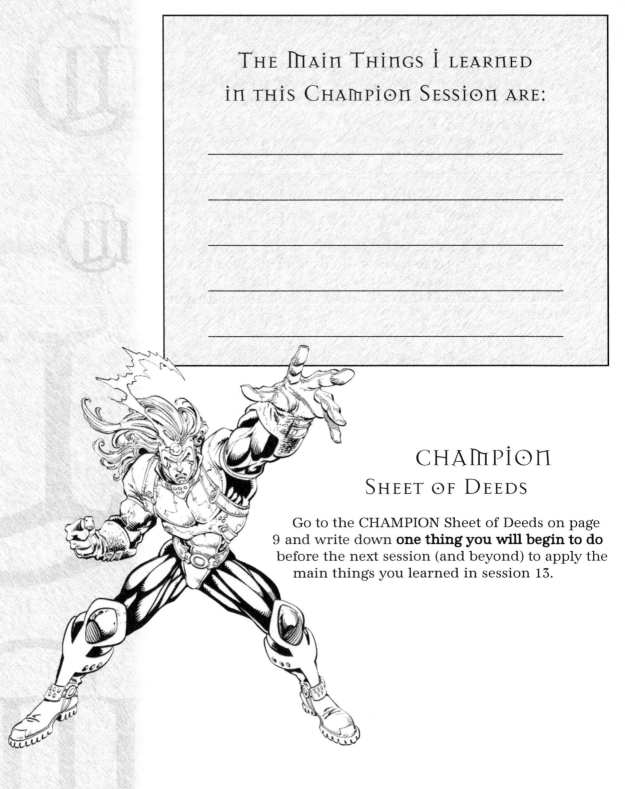

The Main Things I learned in this Champion Session are:

_____

_____

_____

_____

_____

CHAMPION
SHEET OF DEEDS

Go to the CHAMPION Sheet of Deeds on page 9 and write down **one thing you will begin to do** before the next session (and beyond) to apply the main things you learned in session 13.

Your Mission

Complete your mission and CHAMPION Session Prep before you meet for session 14.

Power Verse: Philippians 3:13b-14

Date memorized: _____

Critical Maneuver

This will reinforce what you learned today. Obtain your maneuver instructions from your father.

CHAMPION Sheet of Deeds

Begin to apply your action point from your Sheet of Deeds.

CHAMPION Sesison Prep

Reread episode 14 of *Teknon and the CHAMPION Warriors*, and then complete the questions in session 14 in your *Mission Guide* on your own. **Our next CHAMPION Session will be:**

DATE:

_____

TIME:

_____

PLACE:

_____

◆ Teknon and the CHAMPION Warriors ◆

Courage • Honor • Attitude • Mental toughness • Purity • Integrity • Ownership • Navigation

Session 14:
Back to Back

Champion Characteristics

Integrity and Attitude

Power Verse: Psalm 139:14

I give thanks to You [Lord], for I am fearfully and wonderfully made; wonderful are Your works, and my soul knows it very well.

Discussion Topics

Embracing the strengths and weaknesses of other people
Understanding my own unique bent and value to God's team
Harnessing the power of a diverse team to complete a mission

Mission Debrief

1. Discuss your mission from session 13. What did you learn from your maneuver? How is what you've learned affecting your thinking or behavior?

   _____

2a. As you approach the end of your CHAMPION Training, which of your action points have you been applying from your Sheet of Deeds?

   _____

   _____

2b. Which of your action points have been difficult for you to apply?

   _____

   _____

   _____

It will be important for you to put even greater focus on continuing to apply all of your action points after your CHAMPION Training is complete. Over the next few years, you will have the opportunity to use your action points to develop powerful habits that will advance your development toward courageous manhood. Don't stop the process! Remember what you have learned and continue the process of growth.

3. Recite your power verse (Philippians 3:13b-14) from session 13.

4. Is there an important objective or task that you need to complete? Look again at David's example and the six T's from session 13. Which of these will help you to focus so you can accomplish your objective? Circle them.

   ▲ Target your objective
   ▲ Train yourself for the mission
   ▲ Think of the resources you will need
   ▲ Trust that God will use and empower you
   ▲ Thank God
   ▲ Take action

5. Recite the CHAMPION Warrior Creed (see page 5).

RECONNAISSANCE

1. Review the Map of the Mission on page 8 and determine the team's location in episode 14. They have finally achieved their objective of retrieving the Logos and defeating Magos! But success required tremendous team effort, a great deal of character, and dependence on Pneuma.

2. Review the CHAMPION definitions of **Integrity** and **Attitude**.

_____

_____

_____

_____

_____

_____

3. Why do you think Kratos waited so long to let Teknon use his Hoplon?

_____

_____

Tor explained to Teknon what it means to own the mission: "You gained the head knowledge about becoming a CHAMPION, but not the conviction of heart. For that, you had to face the possibility that no one else would retrieve the Logos unless you stepped in. When you did, the mission not only belonged to us, but to you as well."

4a. What do you think it means to "own" a mission? Is being God's CHAMPION more head knowledge for you or have you been gripped by conviction of the heart? Be honest.

4b. Do you believe God has a mission for you to own? What do you think that mission might be?

⊙ptional Questions

5a. Dolios transformed himself into Teknon's greatest fear in order to defeat him. What was Teknon's greatest fear?

_____

5b. Why do you think this was Teknon's greatest fear?

_____

_____

6. How did Teknon defeat Dolios?

_____

_____

Logos is the Greek term that means "the word." Teknon, his father, and the CHAMPION Warriors risked their lives to retrieve the Logos because of its importance to the people of Basileia. *Logos* is used in the Bible to refer to thoughts and expressions of God Himself delivered in spoken or written form to us. Jesus is also called the Logos because He is the ultimate expression of God's message to man.

7. Why is God's Word, the Bible, so important to us?

_____

_____

_____

_____

8. Tor said, "There is great power in a team." What do you think he meant by that?

_____

_____

_____

9. Kratos instructed the warriors to "watch each other's backs." Why is it important for us to watch out for each other?

_____

_____

_____

_____

Please fill in this chart.

Jot down five words you think describe **Tor**:

1. _____
2. _____
3. _____
4. _____
5. _____

Jot down five words you think describe **Epps**:

1. _____
2. _____
3. _____
4. _____
5. _____

Jot down five words you think describe **Arti**:

1. _____
2. _____
3. _____
4. _____
5. _____

Jot down five words you think describe **Matty**:

1. _____
2. _____
3. _____
4. _____
5. _____

STRATEGY AND TACTICS

DIFFERENT IS DYNAMIC

It's no secret that we all have different "bents." You may like to be the point person, positioning yourself in front of the group as the leader. Or maybe you like to be in the background keeping track of details and helping get things done. Maybe you're a natural salesman: motivating, promoting, and trying to present yourself well in the process.

Does it bother you that you're not the life of the party? Do you wish that you could make friends easier? Does it bother you that you're a cautious person or don't feel comfortable leading?

The point is this: it takes different types of players to make a great team. God uniquely designed each one of us with different strengths and weaknesses. And it's a good thing that everybody isn't alike. What would the world be like if everybody was a CEO ... or an engineer ... or a salesperson ... or a farmer ... or a public speaker?! In God's plan, different is dynamic. Your unique differences provide a dynamic contribution to the mission God has for His team here on earth. To accomplish an important mission, it takes people with different bents and strengths that can fill in each other's gaps and accomplish more as a synchronized unit than any one person could accomplish alone. Be yourself and bring your unique strengths to your family, your church, or whatever team you are a part of—and make it more dynamic!

> *Coming together is a beginning; keeping together is progress; working together is success.*
>
> Henry Ford

HOW ARE YOU BENT?

1. What do you like best about yourself? What do other people seem to like about you?

_____

_____

_____

_____

2. Describe yourself: _____

_____

▲ Are you organized?
▲ Are you the life of the party?
▲ Do you like to be in charge?
▲ Are you a loyal and dedicated friend?

Have you ever considered how unique and important your personal traits are in accomplishing God's plan here on earth? Did you know that God designed you specifically with His perfect plan in mind?

3a. How well does God know you? (Read Psalm 139: 1-12.) What does He know about you?

_____

_____

_____

3b. According to Psalm 139, who created you?

_____

_____

3c. Describe what Psalm 139: 14-18 reveals about your design and uniqueness in God's eyes.

_____

_____

_____

Do you think God makes mistakes? Well, He's God and He doesn't! And according to Psalm 139, God made you just the way you are. And because He made you just the way you are, you are fearfully and wonderfully made in His view! Learn to appreciate who you are and find where you fit on the T-E-A-M.

Let us not give up meeting together, as some are in the habit of doing, but let us encourage one another—and all the more as you see the Day approaching.

Hebrews 10:25
(NIV)

Where Do You Fit On The T-E-A-M?

Complete the following steps to assess your bent and find out where you fit:

Step 1: Under each letter category of the T-E-A-M chart, circle every word or phrase that describes a *consistent* character trait or behavior that you exhibit as you interact *within your family.*

Step 2: Total the number of items you circled in each letter category and write the total in the box at the bottom of each category.

Step 3: Plot the totals from each box on the graph entitled "What's My Bent?" on the next page. Put an "X" on each arrow scale to indicate your score for that category.

Step 4: Discuss your results.

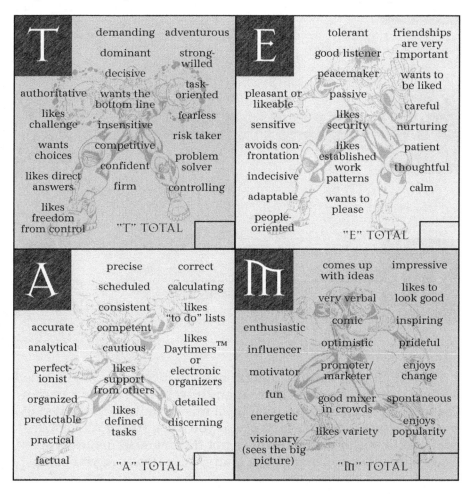

T
demanding   adventurous
dominant   strong-willed
decisive
task-oriented
authoritative   wants the bottom line
likes challenge   insensitive   fearless
risk taker
wants choices   competitive   problem solver
confident
likes direct answers   firm   controlling
likes freedom from control   "T" TOTAL

E
tolerant   friendships are very important
good listener
peacemaker   wants to be liked
pleasant or likeable   passive
careful
sensitive   likes security   nurturing
avoids confrontation   likes established work patterns   patient
indecisive   thoughtful
calm
adaptable   wants to please
people-oriented   "E" TOTAL

A
precise   correct
scheduled   calculating
consistent   likes "to do" lists
accurate   competent
analytical   cautious   likes Daytimers™ or electronic organizers
perfectionist   likes support from others
organized   detailed
likes defined tasks
predictable   discerning
practical
factual   "A" TOTAL

M
comes up with ideas   impressive
likes to look good
very verbal
comic   inspiring
enthusiastic   optimistic   prideful
influencer
promoter/marketer   enjoys change
motivator
fun   good mixer in crowds   spontaneous
energetic
likes variety   enjoys popularity
visionary (sees the big picture)   "M" TOTAL

Based on your ratings, you probably notice that you identified with one of the Warriors more than the others. There's a reason for that. Even though we each have mix of traits, God created us with specific bents. For instance, if you are a strong A like Arti, you don't have to worry if you're not the one who makes everybody laugh like a strong M like Matty. As a strong A, you bring value to the team in other ways, such as your ability to get tasks done completely.

If you are a strong E like Epps, you offer a great deal to the team because of your ability to help calm things down and be a peacemaker. You may admire the leadership skills of a strong T like Tor, but it shouldn't bother you that don't always want to be in charge.

The bottom line: God doesn't want a team made up of clones. God blessed you with a uniquely crafted design for His special purpose in your life. Enjoy the design He gave you and use it to be an integral part of God's team. God wants you on His TEAM—and so do your family and your church!

4. After completing your T-E-A-M assessment, what do you see as some of your strengths?

_____

_____

_____

_____

_____

Stop comparing. Enjoy being you! There's plenty of room in the forest.

Chuck Swindoll

5. Are there strengths or skills that you wish you had? If so, why?

_____

_____

_____

_____

_____

_____

_____

The Main Things I learned in this Champion Session are:

_____

_____

_____

_____

_____

> *In order to have a winner, the team must have a feeling of unity; every player must put the team first—ahead of personal glory.*
>
> Paul "Bear" Bryant

CHAMPION
SHEET OF DEEDS

Go to the CHAMPION Sheet of Deeds on page 9 and write down **one thing you will begin to do** before the next session (and beyond) to apply the main things you learned in session 14.

Your Mission

Complete your mission and CHAMPION Session Prep before you meet for session 15.

Power Verse: Psalm 139:14

Date memorized: _____

Critical Maneuver

This will reinforce what you learned today. Obtain your maneuver instructions from your father.

CHAMPION Sheet of Deeds

Begin to apply your action point from your Sheet of Deeds.

CHAMPION Session Prep

Reread episode 15 of *Teknon and the CHAMPION Warriors*, and then complete the questions in session 15 in your *Mission Guide* on your own. **Our next CHAMPION Session will be:**

DATE:

_____

TIME:

_____

PLACE:

_____

COURAGE • HONOR • ATTITUDE • MENTAL TOUGHNESS • PURITY • INTEGRITY • OWNERSHIP • NAVIGATION

SESSION 15:
CELEBRATION

CHAMPION Characteristics
Navigation and Ownership

POWER VERSE: 2 TIMOTHY 4:7-8A

I have fought the good fight, I have finished the course, I have kept the faith; in the future there is laid up for me the crown of righteousness.

Discussion Topics

Charting your course and accepting your mission
Earning your "wings" so you can begin to fly on your own
Celebrating victories and giving glory to God

Mission Debrief

1. Discuss your mission from session 14. What did you learn from your maneuver? How has your attitude or behavior changed as a result of your maneuver?

   _____

2. One final reminder about your Sheet of Deeds: If you continue to apply all of your action points, it will truly help you to grow toward courageous manhood. Select one of your action points that you will focus on as a priority over the coming weeks. Write it here and put a star by it on your Sheet of Deeds.

   _____

3. Recite your power verse (Psalm 139:14) from session 14.

4. Which of the four mentors do you most resemble in temperament? Who came in second on your list? List what you believe to be three of your greatest strengths from the list of temperament traits.

   _____

   _____

5. Recite the CHAMPION Warrior Creed (see page 5).

Reconnaissance

1. Look again at the Map of the Mission, pause at each location in Teknon's quest, and remember what he learned. Then, review the key things you have learned on your quest for truth. Highlight three important lessons you have learned.

_____

_____

_____

_____

2. Review the CHAMPION definition of **Ownership**.

_____

_____

3. Why do you think Kratos took Teknon's shield back from him?

_____

_____

4. Why do you think Kratos returned Teknon's shield to him during the celebration?

_____

_____

_____

Kratos is a Greek word that means "power and strength." *Teknon* means "child" or "youth." During the CHAMPION Training, you have seen how much you should draw from your dad's strength of character and example. Take note that if you also strive to know God and draw on His power, as Teknon did with Pneuma, you will move from childhood toward becoming a young man of character and courage.

5. What did Kratos say to the group about Teknon during the ceremony?

_____

_____

6. Why do you think it was important for the team to celebrate after its victory on Kairos?

_____

_____

7. Why do you think it was important for Kratos to acknowledge Teknon as a young man to his friends and family?

_____

_____

8. What is the team's continuing mission?

_____

_____

_____

_____

Strategy and Tactics

Earning Your Wings

One of the richest and most significant traditions in our country's history is the awarding of a military pilot's "wings." When a pilot has completed his rigorous training, he is invited to a ceremony and presented with a symbol of the rank, skill, and responsibility that he has earned. When he receives his wings, he is authorized to sit behind the stick of his airplane and fly missions in the service of his country.

But just because he is awarded his wings, a pilot does not stop training. He knows that he must spend his career logging flight time, learning, training, and growing in his knowledge and piloting skills. He wants to become the best pilot that he can be.

Now that you have completed your CHAMPION Training, it's time for you to receive your "wings" and begin the flight into young manhood.

Accept the Challenge

Life was different in the mid-1800s. More than a hundred years ago, Native Americans roamed the plains and mountains of the United States. In those days, teenagers became men almost overnight. Young Indian men knew that when they reached a certain age, they were expected to provide and care for a family. They were also expected to join the rest of the warriors from their tribe in battle.

At what age would you be ready to assume responsibility for a family or be willing to fight an enemy to protect your homeland? If you were a Native American during the mid–1800s, you would have been about 14 years old.

But life is quite different for many teens today. Instead of using their talents and resources to set worthy goals and accomplish great tasks when they're young, they usually settle for trying to get homework done in time to watch TV or get on the Internet. They expect too little of themselves.

Throughout the centuries, there were men who took the first steps down new roads armed with nothing but their own vision.

Ayn Rand

You may not be in this camp, especially after finishing your CHAMPION Training. There are teens who are making a difference in their families and communities. They remember that God is the ultimate source of their talents and resources. They are thankful for what they have and want to be good stewards. They are taking responsibility—helping their parents, working hard at school, reaching out to other people, learning what friendship is all about, setting the right boundaries, and so on. These young people have learned to set high standards for themselves and they are meeting important objectives in life. They seek to know God better and to share Him with others. But remember, there's always room for growth.

An important key to living as a courageous man is to recognize the source of your talents and resources. Once you really grasp Who gave you your abilities and why He gave them to you, your life will never be the same. Let's look at a man in the Bible who learned about the power of God and how God could use him to accomplish mighty things for His people.

WHAT ARE YOU WAITING FOR?

Moses, an Israelite, was adopted by Pharaoh's daughter and raised as a prince in Egypt. But he was enraged about the treatment of his people, who were enslaved and pushed down under the heavy hand of the Egyptians. Initially, he tried to accomplish the mission of freeing his people in his own strength—he killed an Egyptian and had to run away.

Before Moses could become camp counselor to almost seven million people, the leader of the entire nation of Israel, he had to be humbled. He needed time to reflect, to think about who he was, and to learn to depend on God. So God allowed him to shepherd sheep for 40 years in the hills of what became the nation of Israel.

1. According to Exodus 3:1-10, what did God use to get Moses' attention? What did He want Moses to do?

_____

_____

_____

2. When Moses was afraid to carry out the mission God had given him, what did God promise to do for Moses (see Exodus 3:12-21)?

_____

_____

As God continued to speak to Moses out of the burning bush to reveal His plan to deliver the Israelites from Egypt, He told Moses to do something very puzzling.

Read Exodus 4:1-5.
3a. What was in Moses' hand?

_____

3b. What did God tell Moses to do with it the staff?

_____

3c. What did God tell Moses to do next?

_____

3d. Why do you think God told Moses to do these things (see verse 5)?

_____

_____

After 40 years of being a shepherd, God told Moses to lay down his staff. A staff was the most important tool a shepherd owned. It was an instrument he used to guide his sheep through the mountains and it was a weapon he used to ward off wild animals that tried to attack the flock. A shepherd valued his staff even more than Tiger Woods values his driver. Over time, Moses' staff had become like an extension of his arm. He seldom went anywhere without it. The staff was also Moses' security. After all, he had been comfortably hiding out in the wilderness for 40 years. God was asking Moses to take a giant step out his comfort zone.

> *Bring me men to match my mountains. Bring me men to match my plans. Men with empires in their purpose, and new eras in their brains.*
>
> Sam Walter Foss

What kind of man would live where there is no daring? I don't believe in taking foolish chances, but nothing can be accomplished without taking any chances at all.

Charles
Lindbergh

When God asked Moses to lay down his staff, it was like Kratos asking Teknon to return his shield. Moses may not have understood God's reasoning, but he obeyed anyway. God showed Moses the miracles He would perform through the staff and explained that through these miracles the Israelites would know that He had truly appeared to Moses. When God returned the newly designed shepherd's tool to Moses, it was no longer the staff of Moses. It was now the staff of God! The staff became God's instrument to accomplish His mission through Moses.

5. Review the CHAMPION definition of **Navigation**.

_____

_____

Have you grasped through your training that God has a mission for each of us? Do you realize that He has given you the talents and resources you need to accomplish the mission He has for you? When you use your talents for God, and depend on His power, you are exercising good stewardship. You are becoming God's instrument on earth to accomplish His mission.

So what are you waiting for? Get involved in God's mission as a CHAMPION. Trust Him to accomplish the impossible in and through you (that's within God's Ring of Responsibility), but make sure that you're taking responsibility to do all that you can to seek God and pursue excellence in every part of your life (that's within your CHAMPION's Ring). Shouldn't you use the abilities and assets that God has given you to accomplish His goals? God's mission will unfold for you day by day if you will commit to follow Him. It's a great adventure!

One more thing ... it's time to celebrate! You've just completed the entire CHAMPION Training adventure. You've read the episodes, answered the questions, discussed many topics with your dad, and completed the maneuvers and action points. Take time to enjoy this victory and any other victories that you've experienced during your CHAMPION Training. God wants to celebrate the wins in your life and He wants you to celebrate with Him. Thank God for what he has done and for what He will do in and through you as you live your life as a CHAMPION.

The Main Things I learned in this Champion Session are:

_____

_____

_____

_____

And looking at them Jesus said to them, "With people this is impossible, but with God all things are possible."

Matthew 19:26

CHAMPION
Sheet of Deeds

Go to the CHAMPION Sheet of Deeds on page 9 and write down **one thing you will begin to do** before the next session (and beyond) to apply the main things you learned in session 15.

Your Mission

Complete your mission before you meet for your Celebration Ceremony.

Power Verse: 2 Timothy 4:7-8a

Date memorized: _____

Critical Maneuver

This will reinforce what you learned today. Obtain your maneuver instructions from your father.

Champion Sheet of Deeds

Continue to apply your action points from your Sheet of Deeds.

Celebration Ceremony

If your dad is planning a celebration ceremony for you, write down the specifics here.

Dad, celebrate your son's accomplishment in completing his CHAMPION Training with a ceremony! Refer to chapter 4 of your *Mentor Guide* for practical tips on putting together an effective ceremony for your son. My Celebration Ceremony will be:

Date: _____

Time: _____

Place: _____

Congratulations on a job well done!

Nike® says it, and we buy into it. You look at the "swoosh," as Nike calls it, and the phrase comes to your mind. You hear it in commercials, you see it on the billboards, and it's plastered on millions of shirts, shoes, and shorts. Over a period of time, we come to believe it only because some well-paid marketing wizards found a creative way to sell more products. Now, why don't we say that phrase all together? Ready, one, two, three:

JUST DO IT!

If only all of life were as easy as this slogan makes it sound. The truth is, life is a lot harder than selling trendy clothing. In fact, we can't "just do it" on our own when it comes to living a life in which we're unconditionally loved, eternally protected, and fully satisfied.

We need power to do that—a lot of power. Power that can only come from an all-powerful God who wants us to relate to Him on a personal level. Only those people who know Him and seek Him have access to God's unlimited power. He offers it as a free gift that we receive through faith in His Son, Jesus Christ.

God created us to have an abundant life now and for eternity. But He did not create us like androids that would automatically love and follow Him. He gave us a will and freedom to choose our eternal destination. What will you choose?

Are you 100% sure that, when you die, you are going to heaven? Why do you say that?

Mark on the following scale, how sure you are that you have a personal relationship with God, through Jesus Christ:

Not at all sure   1   2   3   4   5   Very sure

How do you know?

_____

_____

Would you like to be 100% fully sure that you have a personal relationship with God that will guarantee your passport to heaven?

_____

_____

God's power is experienced by knowing God personally and by growing in our relationship with Him. God has provided the power necessary to fulfill His purposes and to carry out His mission for our lives. God is so eager to establish a personal, loving relationship with you that He has already made all the arrangements. He is patiently and lovingly waiting for you to respond to His invitation.

The major barrier that prevents us from knowing God personally is ignorance of who God is and what he has done for us. The following four principles will help you discover how to know God personally and experience the abundant life He promised.

GOD LOVES YOU AND CREATED YOU TO KNOW HIM PERSONALLY.

a. God loves you.

"For God so loved the world, that He gave His only begotten Son, that whoever believes in Him should not perish but have eternal life." John 3:16

b. God wants you to know Him.

"Now this is eternal life: that they may know You, the only true God, and Jesus Christ, whom You have sent." John 17:3 (NIV)

What prevents us from knowing God personally?

WE ARE SINFUL AND SEPARATED FROM GOD, SO WE CANNOT KNOW HIM PERSONALLY OR EXPERIENCE HIS LOVE AND POWER.

(Author's Note: The word sin *confuses a lot of people. The word* sin *comes from a Greek term that was used in archery. When archers shot at the target, the distance by which their arrow missed the bull's-eye was called sin. That distance represented the degree to which the archer missed the mark of perfection. When we miss God's mark of perfection, it's called sin too. And because of sin, there is a wall that separates us from a perfectly holy God. Through the years, people have tried many things to break through that wall. Money, power, and fame are just a few of the things people have tried. None of them have worked. We all fall short of God's perfection.)*

a. Man is sinful.

"For all have sinned and fall short of the glory of God." Romans 3:23

b. Man is separated.

For the wages of sin is death [spiritual separation from God]. Romans 6:23a

How can the canyon between God and man be bridged?

APPENDIX A: JUST DO IT!

3 JESUS CHRIST IS THE ONLY PROVISION FOR MAN'S SIN. THROUGH HIM ALONE WE CAN KNOW GOD PERSONALLY AND EXPERIENCE GOD'S LOVE.

a. God became a man through the Person of Jesus Christ.

But the angel said to them, "Do not be afraid; for behold, I bring you good news of great joy which will be for all the people; for today in the city of David there has been born for you a Savior, who is Christ the Lord." Luke 2:10-11

b. He died in our place.

"But God demonstrates His own love toward us in that while we were yet sinners, Christ died for us." Romans 5:8

c. He rose from the dead.

"Christ died for our sins according to the Scriptures ... He was buried ... He was raised on the third day according to the Scriptures ... He appeared to Peter, then to the twelve. After that He appeared to more than five hundred." 1 Corinthians 15:3b-6a

d. He is the only way to God.

"Jesus said to him, 'I am the way, and the truth, and the life; no one comes to the Father but through Me.'" John 14:6

It is not enough to know these truths ...

4 WE MUST INDIVIDUALLY RECEIVE JESUS CHRIST AS SAVIOR AND LORD; THEN WE CAN KNOW GOD PERSONALLY AND EXPERIENCE HIS LOVE.

a. We must receive Christ.

"But as many as received Him, to them He gave the right to become children of God, even to those who believe in His name." John 1:12

b. We must receive Christ through faith.

"For by grace you have been saved through faith; and that not of yourselves, it is the gift of God; not as a result of works, so that no one may boast." Ephesians 2:8-9

c. When we receive Christ we experience a new birth (read John 3:1-8).

d. We must receive Christ by personal invitation.

"I am the door; if anyone enters through Me, he will be saved ..." John 10:9

Receiving Christ involves turning to God from self (repentance) and trusting Christ to come into our lives to forgive us of our sins and to make us what He wants us to be. Just to agree intellectually that Jesus Christ is the Son of God and that He died on the cross for our sins is not enough. Nor is it enough to have an emotional experience. We receive Jesus Christ by faith, as an act of our will.

These two circles represent two kinds of lives:

Which circle best represents your life?

Which circle would you like to have represent your life?

You Can Receive Christ Right Now By Faith Through Prayer

God knows your heart and is not so concerned with your words as He is with the attitude of your heart. Here is a suggested life-changing prayer:

Lord Jesus, I want to know You personally. Thank you for dying on the cross for my sins. I open the door of my life and receive You as my Savior and Lord. Thank you for forgiving me of my sins and giving me eternal life. Take control of the throne of my life. Make me the kind of person You want me to be.

If you sincerely prayed this prayer, you can know with 100% certainty that Christ is in your life and He is there to stay (Hebrews 13:5). So, you don't have to "just do it". God has already done it for you. You may or may not feel like it now, but this is the most important day of your life. To remember this major event in your life when you joined God's family, sign and date this page.

_____   _____
             Signature   *Date*

What Are the Results of Placing Your Faith in Jesus Christ?

The Bible says:

1. Jesus Christ came into your life (Colossians 1:27).

2. Your sins were forgiven (Colossians 1:14).

3. You became a child of God (John 1:12)

4. You received eternal life (John 5:24).

5. You have the power to pursue intimacy with God (Romans 5:5).

6. You began the great adventure, the mission, for which God created you (John 10:10, 2 Corinthians 5:17, and 1 Thessalonians 5:18).

CHAMPION
TRAINING ADVENTURE
PROGRAM

For other *Teknon and the Champion Warriors* resources check out our Web site at www.generationsofvirtue.org for:

▲ Character illustrations and descriptions

▲ Downloadable CHAMPION Creed and Code

▲ Downloadable sample forms

▲ New ideas for CHAMPION Training

▲ Great links and more!

Media Evaluation Report

When using movies, audio cassettes, and books for action points, consider asking your son to write a one-page report that answers the following questions.

1. How would you summarize the movie, audio cassette, or book?

2. What is the main point of the story?

3. Who is the hero? Who is the villain?

4. What skills or gifts did the hero rely on to succeed?

5. Do you agree with the hero's behavior and the methods he used? If not, what would you have done in his place?

6. What CHAMPION characteristics did the hero exhibit?

7. As you think of this story, name one story or passage from the Bible that it reminds you of.

8. How do the messages in this apply to me?

9. List other special questions identified in the *Mentor Guide* for each session:

●

●

●

Acknowledgements

Putting together an integrated program with a fiction novel for teens, an interactive training guide, and a comprehensive how-to manual for dads has been quite a challenge. There are a number of people I wish to thank for helping me to make *Teknon and the CHAMPION Warriors* a reality.

I would like to thank Neal and Ida Jean Sapp, Sam Bartlett, Sheri and Jack McGill, Dr. Gilbert Chandler, Martin Shipman, Don Jacobs, Roger Berry, Nick and Amy Repak, Michael Hohmann, Steve Bruton, Sergio Cariello, Rick Blanchette, Donald Joy, and Stephen Sorenson for their invaluable input and encouragement.

I also appreciate the dedicated team at FamilyLife for the theological, editorial, and design direction. This team includes Jerry McCall, Blair Wright, David Sims, Bob Anderson, Anne Wooten, and Fran Taylor.

My heartfelt thanks are extended to Ben Colter who, through his hard work and creative editing expertise, has helped to transform this material into an adventurous, user-friendly training program that we hope will greatly benefit both you and your son.

I want to thank my wife, Ellen, for striving with me to raise our children with strong character and for enduring the process of developing these materials. Last, but not least, I want to acknowledge my children, Katie, Kimberly, Kyle, and especially Casey for giving me encouragement and inspiration during the creative development of the CHAMPION Training adventure program. Thanks, kids!

Notes

Session 6

Original source unknown for "Nasty as We Wanna Be" article.

About the Author

Brent Sapp is a first time writer from Orlando. When his older son, Casey, was nearing the teen years, Brent conceived a fun program that he and some friends pursued together with their sons. They called themselves CHAMPION Warriors. The program caught on in Florida and in other areas of the country. From this successful venture, Brent has adapted the key principles of a CHAMPION into a futuristic adventure novel for teen boys. He has also developed an interactive character-building program for fathers to use with their sons as a companion resource to *Teknon and the CHAMPION Warriors*.

Brent and his wife, Ellen, have four children (Casey, 16; Katie, 14; Kimberly, 12; and Kyle, 9). Brent is a graduate of Florida State University and has an MBA from Rollins College. He has worked as a medical sales representative for the past 16 years. When not representing medical and surgical equipment, Brent volunteers with Ellen to help bring the FamilyLife Marriage Conference to Orlando and also to prepare dozens of young couples for marriage each year at Northland Community Church.

About the Illustrator

Sergio Cariello is the talented free-lance illustrator behind the characters of *Teknon and the CHAMPION Warriors*. He also draws such well-known icons as Superman and Batman for DC Comics. In addition, he teaches at the prestigious Joe Kubert School of Cartooning and Animation. Sergio lives in South River, N.J., with his wife, Luzia.

Notes

Notes

Notes

Notes

NOTES

Notes

NOTES

NOTES

Notes

Notes

Notes

Notes

Notes

Notes

Notes

_____

_____

_____

_____

_____

_____

_____

_____

_____

_____

_____

_____

CPSIA information can be obtained at www.ICGtesting.com
Printed in the USA
BVOW09s1649030815

411548BV00021B/992/P